COMPUTER SCIENCE, TECHNOLOGY AND APPLICATIONS

C PROGRAMMING FOR JUNIORS

COMPUTER SCIENCE, TECHNOLOGY AND APPLICATIONS

Additional books in this series can be found on Nova's website under the Series tab.

Additional e-books in this series can be found on Nova's website under the e-book tab.

COMPUTER SCIENCE, TECHNOLOGY AND APPLICATIONS

C PROGRAMMING FOR JUNIORS

S. ANANDAMURUGAN

New York

Copyright © 2014 by Nova Science Publishers, Inc.

All rights reserved. No part of this book may be reproduced, stored in a retrieval system or transmitted in any form or by any means: electronic, electrostatic, magnetic, tape, mechanical photocopying, recording or otherwise without the written permission of the Publisher.

For permission to use material from this book please contact us:
Telephone 631-231-7269; Fax 631-231-8175
Web Site: http://www.novapublishers.com

NOTICE TO THE READER

The Publisher has taken reasonable care in the preparation of this book, but makes no expressed or implied warranty of any kind and assumes no responsibility for any errors or omissions. No liability is assumed for incidental or consequential damages in connection with or arising out of information contained in this book. The Publisher shall not be liable for any special, consequential, or exemplary damages resulting, in whole or in part, from the readers' use of, or reliance upon, this material. Any parts of this book based on government reports are so indicated and copyright is claimed for those parts to the extent applicable to compilations of such works.

Independent verification should be sought for any data, advice or recommendations contained in this book. In addition, no responsibility is assumed by the publisher for any injury and/or damage to persons or property arising from any methods, products, instructions, ideas or otherwise contained in this publication.

This publication is designed to provide accurate and authoritative information with regard to the subject matter covered herein. It is sold with the clear understanding that the Publisher is not engaged in rendering legal or any other professional services. If legal or any other expert assistance is required, the services of a competent person should be sought. FROM A DECLARATION OF PARTICIPANTS JOINTLY ADOPTED BY A COMMITTEE OF THE AMERICAN BAR ASSOCIATION AND A COMMITTEE OF PUBLISHERS.

Additional color graphics may be available in the e-book version of this book.

Library of Congress Cataloging-in-Publication Data

Anandamurugan, S., author.
 C programming for juniors / S. Anandamurugan (Kongu Engineering College, Perundurai, Tamilnadu, India).
    pages cm. -- (Computer science, technology and applications)
 Includes index.
 ISBN: 978-1-63321-198-8 (softcover)
 1. C (Computer program language) I. Title.
 QA76.73.C15A474 2014
 005.13'3--dc23
                                    2014020785

Published by Nova Science Publishers, Inc. † New York

CONTENTS

Preface		vii
Author Profile		ix
Acknowledgments		xi
Chapter 1	Introduction to C	1
Chapter 2	Data Types, Constants and Variables	5
Chapter 3	Getting Started with Basics	11
Chapter 4	Operators and Expressions	15
Chapter 5	Program Control	27
Chapter 6	Standard Input/Output	37
Chapter 7	Functions	41
Chapter 8	Strings and Arrays	49
Chapter 9	Structures, Union, Bit Fields	55
Chapter 10	Pointers	67
Chapter 11	File Input/Output	85
Chapter 12	Dynamic Memory Allocation	97
Appendix A. Exercises for Cruising Your Technical Mind		103
Appendix B. Miscellaneous Question and Answers		105
Appendix C. C Questions		107
Index		173

PREFACE

This book gives a detailed introduction to C Programming concepts. It is very useful for those who are new to C. The aim of this book is to give maximum guidance to the students, faculty, research scholars and people working with computers. Suggestions for improvement will be appreciated and incorporated.

AUTHOR PROFILE

Dr. S. ANANDAMURUGAN obtained his Bachelor's degree in Electrical and Electronics Engineering from "Maharaja Engineering College - Avinashi" under Bharathiyar University and Masters Degree in Computer Science and Engineering from "Arulmigu Kalasalingam College of Engineering – Krishnan Koil" under Madurai Kamaraj University. He completed his Ph.D in Wireless Sensor Networks from Anna University, Chennai. He has 13 years of teaching experience. Currently he is working as an Assistant Professor (Selection Grade) in the department of Information Technology in Kongu Engineering College, Perundurai. He is a life member of ISTE, CSI & ACEEE. He has received "Best Staff" award for the year 2007-08. He has authored more than 70 books. He has Published 20 papers in International and National Journals and 10 Papers in International and National Conferences. His area of interest includes Sensor Networks and Green Computing. He is an Editorial Board Member of the International Journal of Computing Academic Research (IJCAR). He has organized 1CSIR sponsored seminar for the benefit of faculty members and students. He has attended about 40 Seminars, FDP's, and Workshops organized by various Engineering colleges.

ACKNOWLEDGMENTS

I would like to express my sincere gratitude to Thiru. V.K. Muthusamy, Correspondent, Kongu Engineering College, for having provided me with all necessary facilities to undertake this work.

I feel extremely grateful for the strong support which I have received from Prof. S. Kuppuswami, Principal, and Prof. S. Balamurugan, Dean, School of Communication and Computer Sciences.

I would like to thank Dr. S. Varadhaganapathy, Head of the Department, Information Technology, Kongu Engineering College for his commendable help and support during this work.

I would like to courey my special thanks from the bottom of my heart to my admirable parents R.Selvaraj, S.Annammal, wife Dr. S. Renukadevi, lovable son A. Shrikarthick, for their moral support which I cannot adequately explain in a few words.

I extend my sincere thanks to all my colleagues for their comments and suggestions. Finally, I would like to thank everyone who have encouraged me at every stage in the successful completion of the book.

Dr. S. Anandamurugan

Chapter 1

INTRODUCTION TO C

ABSTRACT

This chapter gives an overview of the C language after providing the reader with an outline of its brief history. The role of interpreter and compiler is also explained.

Outline

- Why is C needed?
- What is C?
- Why to use C?

1.1. WHY IS C NEEDED?

As with previous languages like B and COBOL (used for mainframes) there were a couple of problems and some facilities were missing and to overcome these problems the age and the era of the "C" language started.

1.2. WHAT IS C?

C is a programming language developed at AT & T's Bell Laboratories of USA in 1972. It was designed and written by a man named Dennis Ritchie. In the late seventies C began to replace the more familiar languages of that time like PL/I, ALGOL, etc. No one really pushed C.

1.3. WHY TO USE C?

C was initially used for system development work, in particular for programs that make-up the operating system. C was adopted as a system development language because it produced codes that ran nearly as fast as the codes written in assembly language. For example, when we need to write any of the Kernel in the operating system the base for it will be C, C++. Some examples of the use of C are:

- Operating Systems
- Language Compilers
- Assemblers
- Print Spoolers
- Language Interpreters

Sample Program:

Having seen something about the terms and the conditions of the "C" language, let's now go for a sample set of the program.
EX:

1. #include<stdio.h>
2. #include<conio.h>
3. void main()
4. {
5. clrscr();
6. printf("Hello and welcome to the C Language..!!!! \n");
7. }

What's Up:

The first two lines are to include all the necessary functionalities in to your code. After it, soon we would be seeing the "void main()" statement.. It is the main entry point of all C program. Without the inclusion of the main() you cannot do anything!!!

1. After that line you can see the function namely "clrscr();" . It is used to clear the screen since it may contain some other unnecessary codes.
2. A normal print statement which gets used to print the line on the screen

CONCLUDING REMARKS

In this chapter you have studied the history and basics of C language. You have studied the role of an interpreter, compiler and the differences between them.

Chapter 2

DATA TYPES, CONSTANTS AND VARIABLES

ABSTRACT

The fundamentals of C are explained in this chapter. The reader is introduced to different data types like characters, digits, white space, and special characters. Various delimiters, constants, variables and data types are described. Intializations of a variable, type conversions, etc. are narrated.
Outline

- Data types in C Language
- User defined data types
- Size and Range of data types on 16 bit machine
- Declaration of storage class
- Typecasting

2.1. DATA TYPES IN C LANGUAGE

A programming language is proposed to help the programmer to process certain kinds of data and to provide useful outputs. The task of data processing is accomplished by executing a series of commands called program. A program usually contains different types of data types (integer, float, character etc.) and need to store the values being used in the program. C language is rich in data types. C programmers have to employ proper data type as per the requirement.

C has different data types for different requirements and can be broadly classified as:

1. Primary data types
2. Secondary data types (Derived Data types)
3. User Defined data types

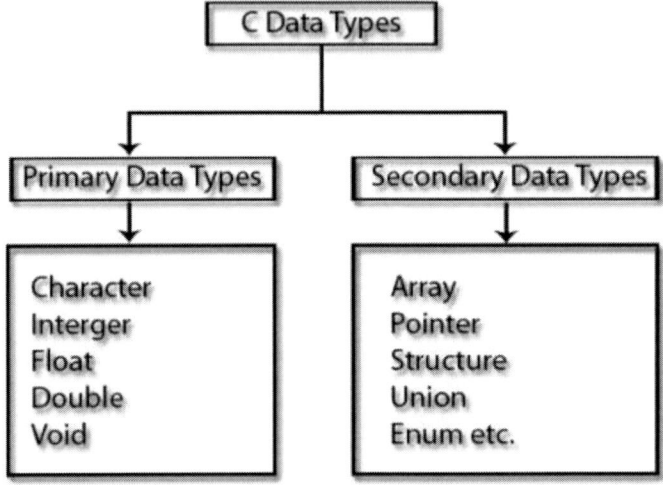

Of them all, the UDT (User Defined Data Types) are the most important ones. So we need to take a look at them!

2.2. USER DEFINED DATA TYPES

C language supports a feature where the user can define an identifier that characterizes an existing data type. This user defined data type identifier can later be used to declare variables. In short its purpose is to redefine the name of an existing data-type.

Syntax:
typedef <type> <identifier>; like
typedef int number;

Example:
typedef int Units;
typedef float average;

Data Types, Constants and Variables

Here Units symbolize int and average symbolizes float. They can be later used to declare variables as follows:

Units dept1, dept2;
Average section1, section2;

Therefore dept1 and dept2 are indirectly declared as integer data type and section1 and section2 are indirectly declared or seen as float data type. The second type of user defined data type is called enumerated data type which is defined as follows.
Enum identifier {value1, value2 .... Value n};

The identifier is a user defined enumerated data type which can be used to declare variables that have one of the values enclosed within braces. After the definition we can declare variables to be of this 'new' type as below.

enum identifier V1, V2, V3, ... Vn

The enumerated variables V1, V2....Vn can have only one of the values such as value1, value2 ..... or valuen.

Example:

enum day {Monday, Tuesday, ... Sunday};
enum day week_st, week end;
week_st = Monday;
week_end = Friday;
if(wk_st == Tuesday)
week_en = Saturday;

2.3. SIZE AND RANGE OF DATA TYPES ON 16 BIT MACHINE

Note that the following size will definitely depend on the type of the compiler and the architecture of the system. The following values are based on the 32-Bit architecture and the 16-Bit compiler edition. So, C compiler widely in usage is mostly 16Bit and there is no need to worry about the differences in the size of the data type now!

type	SIZE (Bits)	Range
Char or Signed Char	8	-128 to 127
Unsigned Char	8	0 to 255
Int or Signed int	16	-32768 to 32767
type	SIZE (Bits)	Range
Unsigned int	16	0 to 65535
Short int or Signed short int	8	-128 to 127
Unsigned short int	8	0 to 255
Long int or signed long int	32	-2147483648 to 2147483647
Unsigned long int	32	0 to 4294967295
Float	32	3.4 e-38 to 3.4 e+38
Double	64	1.7e-308 to 1.7e+308
Long Double	80	3.4 e-4932 to 3.4 e+4932

2.4. DECLARATION OF STORAGE CLASS

Variables in C include not only the data type but also the storage class that provides information about their location and visibility. The storage class divides the portion of the program within which the variables are recognized. The storage classes are classified as below:

auto: It is a local variable known only to the function
static: Local variable which exist and retain its value
extern: Global variable known to all functions in the file register: Social variables which are stored in the register
As you know, these storage classes are useful in different and in appropriate environments!!!

2.5. TYPE CASTING

Converting an expression of a given type into another type is known as *type-casting*. We have already seen some ways to type cast:

1. Implicit Conversion

Implicit conversions do not require any operator. They are automatically performed when a value is copied to a compatible type. For example:

Data Types, Constants and Variables

Short b=2222
Int a=b

Here, the value of "a" has been promoted from short to int and there is no need to specify any type-casting operator. This is known as standard conversion. Standard conversions affect fundamental data types, and allow conversions such as the conversions between numerical types (short to int, int to float, double to int...), and some pointer conversions. Some of these conversions may imply a loss of precision, which the compiler can signal with a warning. This can be avoided with an explicit conversion.

2. Explicit Conversion

C++ is a strong-typed language. Many conversions, specially those that imply a different interpretation of the value, require an explicit conversion. We have already seen two notations for explicit type conversion: functional and c-like casting:

Short b=2000;
int a= (int)b;

CONCLUDING REMARKS

The reader is now exposed to the additional fundamentals of C. These things are absolutely essential for writing programs. The reader is made aware of the following points.

- Different types of characters like letters, digits, white space, and special characters
- Various delimeters used with C statements, keywords and identifiers
- Different constants, variables, and data types
- Rules for defining variables and initializing them
- Type conversion of variable

Chapter 3

GETTING STARTED WITH BASICS

ABSTRACT

This chapter gives the structure of the C language. Various sections of the program, together with rules for writing a C program are presented. Outline:

- Structure of C program
- Sample Programs
- Programming Rules

3.1. STRUCTURE OF C PROGRAM

.....Documentation Section
.....
.....Link Section
.....
.....Definition Section
.....
.....Global declaration Section
.....
.....main () function section
.....{
..........Declaration Section
.....
..........Executable Section

```
.....}
.....Sub-program Section
.....function1
.....{
..........Statements
.....}
.....function2
.....{
..........Statements
.....}
.....function3
.....{
..........Statements
.....}
```

Every C program will consist of one or more functions. A function is nothing but a group or sequence of C statements that are executed together. Each C program function performs a specific task.

The 'main()' function is the most important function and must be present in every C program. The execution of a C program begins in the main() function.

Document Section describes complete program details using comment lines.

Link sections include header file section. Each header file by default is extended with .h and the header file should be included using # include <stdio.h>. Whereas <stdio.h> file is included that is all the definitions and prototypes of functions which is defined in file ware available in current program. This file is also compiled with the original program.

Definition Section: Symbolic constants (# define) which define the values cannot be changed.

Global Declaration section: This section declares some variables that are used in more than function. This section must be declared put of all variables.

Function Section: Main function is the most important part of C program. The program execution starts from open brace ({) and ends with closing brace (}). Between these two braces the program should show the declaration and executable part.

Declaration part: it declares the entire variables that are used in executable part. The initializations of variables are also done in this section. Initializations mean providing initial value of the variable.

Executable part: This part contains the statements following the declaration of the variables. This part contains a set of statements or a single statement. These statements are enclosed between braces.

Sub program Section: It means user defined function (created by user) with a set of statement only call.

// → Single line statement
/*→ Multiple line statement */

3.2. SAMPLE PROGRAM

```
#include <stdio.h>
main( )
{
int a,b,c;
a=10; b=20;
c=a+b;
printf("%d"'c);
}
```

3.3. PROGRAMMING RULES

1. All statements should be written in lower case letters. Upper case letters are only used for symbolic constants.
2. Blank spaces may be inserted between the words. This improves the readability of the statements. However it is not used while declaring a variable, keyword, constant and function.
3. It is not necessary to fix the position of the statement in the program. The programmer can write the statement anywhere between the two braces following the declaration part. The user can also write one or more statements in one line separating them with a semi colon (;) hence it is often called a free from language.

A=b*c ; d=b*c;   or   a=b+c; d=b*c;

The opening and closing braces should be balanced.

CONCLUDING REMARKS

This chapter outlines the various sections of a program and rules that can be adopted while writing a program.

Chapter 4

OPERATORS AND EXPRESSIONS

ABSTRACT

This chapter covers various arithmetic, logical and relational operators, which are essential for the writing and execution of programs. The precedence of the operators in arithmetic operations is explained. The conditional and comma operators and programs based on them are described in this chapter. The use of OR, AND, NOT and XOR operators, Bitwise operators and their usage are highlighted.

Outline:

- Operators Introduction
- Arithmetic Operators
- Relational Operators
- Logical Operators
- Assignment Operators
- Increment and Decrement Operators
- Conditional or Ternary Operators
- Bitwise Operators
- Special Operators

4.1. OPERATORS INTRODUCTION

An operator is a symbol which helps the user to command the computer to do certain mathematical or logical manipulations. Operators are used in C language program to operate on data and variables. C has a rich set of operators which can be classified as

1. Arithmetic Operators
2. Relational Operators
3. Logical Operators
4. Assignment Operators
5. Increment and Decrement Operators
6. Conditional Operators
7. Bitwise Operators
8. Special Operators

4.1.1. Arithmetic Operators

All the basic arithmetic operations can be carried out in C. All the operators have almost the same meaning as in other languages. Both unary and binary operations are available in C language. Unary operations operate on a single operand, therefore the number 5 when operated by unary – will have the value –5.

Operator	Meaning
+	Addition or Unary Plus
–	Subtraction or Unary Minus
*	Multiplication
/	Division
%	Modulus Operator

Examples of Arithmetic Operators

x + y
x - y
-x + y
a * b + c
-a * b etc.,

here a, b, c, x, y are known as operands. The modulus operator is a special operator in C language which evaluates the remainder of the operands after division.

4.1.2. Relational Operators

Often it is required to compare the relationship between operands and bring out a decision and program accordingly. This is when the relational operator comes into the picture. C supports the following relational operators.

Operator	Meaning
<	is less than
<=	is less than or equal to
>	is greater than
>=	is greater than or equal to
==	is equal to
!=	is not equal to

If it is required to compare the marks of 2 students, or the salary of 2 persons, we can compare them using relational operators.

A simple relational expression contains only one relational operator and takes the following form.

exp1 relational operator exp2

Where exp1 and exp2 are expressions, which may be simple constants, variables or a combination of them.

4.1.3. Logical Operators

C has the following logical operators; they compare or evaluate logical and relational expressions.

Operator	Meaning
&&	Logical AND
||	Logical OR
!	Logical NOT

Logical AND (&&):

This operator is used to evaluate 2 conditions or expressions with relational operators simultaneously. If both the expressions to the left and to the right of the logical operator are true then the whole compound expression is true.

&& OPERATOR

A	B	A && B
True	True	True
True	False	False
False	True	False
False	False	False

Example: a > b && x = = 10

The expression to the left is a > b and that on the right is x == 10 then the whole expression is true only if both expressions are true i.e., if a is greater than b and x is equal to 10.

Logical OR (||):

The logical OR is used to combine 2 expressions and the condition evaluates to true if any one of the 2 expressions is true.

|| OPERATOR

A	B	A || B
True	True	True
True	False	True
False	True	True
False	False	False

Example: a < m || a < n

The expression evaluates to true if any one of them is true or if both of them are true. It evaluates to true if a is less than either m or n and when a is less than both m and n.

Logical NOT (!):

The logical not operator takes a single expression and evaluates to true if the expression is false and evaluates it to false if the expression is true. In other words it just reverses the value of the expression.

For example: !(x >= y) the NOT expression evaluates to true only if the value of x is neither greater than or equal to y.

4.1.4. Assignment Operators

The Assignment Operator evaluates an expression on the right of the expression and substitutes it to the value or variable on the left of the expression.

Example: x = a + b

Here the value of a + b is evaluated and substituted to the variable x. In addition, C has a set of shorthand assignment operators of the form

var oper = exp;

Here var is a variable, exp is an expression and oper is a C binary arithmetic operator. The operator oper = is known as shorthand assignment operator

Example: x + = 1 is same as x = x + 1

The commonly used shorthand assignment operators are as follows:

Statement with simple assignment operator	Statement with shorthand operator
a = a + 1	a += 1
a = a – 1	a -= 1
a = a * (n+1)	a *= (n+1)
a = a / (n+1)	a /= (n+1)
a = a % b	a %= b

4.1.5. Increment and Decrement Operators

++variable name and variable name++ mean the same thing when they form statements independently, they behave differently when they are used in expression on the right hand side of an assignment statement.
Consider the following

m = 5;
y = ++m; (prefix or pre increment)
In this case the value of y and m would be 6.

Suppose if we rewrite the previous statement as...

m = 5;
y = m++; (post fix or post increment),

then the value of y will be 5 and that of m will be 6. A prefix operator first adds 1 to the operand and then the result is assigned to the variable on the left. On the other hand, a postfix operator first assigns the value to the variable on the left and then increments the operand. (Same as pre and post decrement operator).

4.1.6. Conditional or Ternary Operator

The conditional operator consists of 2 symbols, question mark (?) and colon(:) The syntax for a ternary operator is as follows:

exp1 ? exp2 : exp3

The ternary operator works as follows :
exp1 is evaluated first. If the expression is true then exp2 is evaluated & its value becomes the value of the expression. If exp1 is false, exp3 is evaluated and its value becomes the value of the expression. Note that only one of the expressions is evaluated.
For example:

a = 10;
b = 15;
x = (a > b) ? a : b

Here x will be assigned to the value of b. The condition follows that the expression is false therefore b is assigned to x.

void main()
{
int i,j,larger;
printf ("Input 2 integers : ");
scanf("%d %d",&i, &j);
larger = i > j ? i : j;

printf("The largest of two numbers is %d \n", larger);
}
Output:
Input 2 integers : 34 45
The largest of two numbers is 45

4.1.7. Bitwise Operators

C has the distinction of supporting special operators known as bitwise operators for manipulation of data at bit level. A bitwise operator operates on each bit of data. Those operators are used for testing, complementing or shifting bits to the right or left. Bitwise operators may not be applied to a float or double.

The Bitwise operator works on bits and performs a bit by bit operation. Assume if B = 60; and B = 13; Now in binary format they will be as follows:

A = 0011 1100
B = 0000 1101

A&B = 0000 1000
A|B = 0011 1101
A^B = 0011 0001
~A = 1100 0011
A>>=2 = 00001111
B<<=2 = 00110100

Following are the Bitwise operators supported by C language:

Operator	Description	Example
&	Binary AND Operator copies a bit to the result if it exists in both operands.	(A & B) will give 12 which is 0000 1100
|	Binary OR Operator copies a bit if it exists in either operand.	(A | B) will give 61 which is 0011 1101
^	Binary XOR Operator copies the bit if it is set in one operand but not both.	(A ^ B) will give 49 which is 0011 0001
~	Binary Ones Complement Operator is unary and has the effect of 'flipping' bits.	(~A) will give -60 which is 1100 0011
<<	Binary Left Shift Operator. The left operands value is moved left by the number of bits specified by the right operand.	A << 2 will give 240 which is 1111 0000
>>	Binary Right Shift Operator. The left operands value is moved right by the number of bits specified by the right operand.	A >> 2 will give 15 which is 0000 1111

The shift operators perform appropriate shift by operator on the right to the operator on the left. The right operator must be positive. The vacated bits are filled with zero.

For example: x << 2 shifts the bits in x by 2 places to the left.
if x = 00000010 (binary) or 2 (decimal)
then:
x >>= 2 => x = 00000000 or just 0 (decimal)
Also: if x = 00000010 (binary) or 2 (decimal)
then
x <<= 2 => x = 00001000 or 8 (decimal)

Therefore a shift left is equivalent to a multiplication by 2. Similarly a shift right is equal to division by 2. Shifting is much faster than actual multiplication (*) or division (/) by 2. So if you want fast multiplications or division by 2 use shifts.

To illustrate many points of bitwise operators let us write a function, Bitcount, that counts bits set to 1 in an 8 bit number (unsigned char) passed as an argument to the function.

This function illustrates many C program points:

for loop is not used for simple counting operation.
x >>= 1 => x = x>> 1;
for loop will repeatedly shift right x until x becomes 0
use expression evaluation of x & 01 to control if
x & 01 masks of 1st bit of x if this is 1 then count++.

4.1.8. Special Operators

C supports some special operators of interest such as comma operator, sizeof operator, pointer operators (& and *) and member selection operators (. and ->). The sizeof and the comma operators are discussed here. The remaining operators are discussed in the forth coming chapters.

The Comma Operator:

The comma operator can be used to link related expressions together. A comma-linked list of expressions is evaluated left to right and the value of the right most expression is the value of the combined expression.

For example the statement: value = (x = 10, y = 5, x + y);
First assigns 10 to x and 5 to y and finally assigns 15 to value. Since comma has the lowest precedence in operators the parenthesis is necessary. Some examples of comma operator are

In for loops: for (n=1, m=10, n <=m; n++,m++)
In while loops: While (c=getchar(), c != '10')
Exchanging values: t = x, x = y, y = t;
The size of Operator:
The operator sizeof gives the size of the data type or variable in terms of bytes occupied in the memory. The operand may be a variable, a constant or a data type qualifier.
Example:-

m = sizeof (sum);
n = sizeof (long int);
k = sizeof (235L);

The size of operator is normally used to determine the lengths of arrays and structures when their sizes are not known to the programmer. It is also used to allocate memory space dynamically to variables during the execution of the program.
Example program that employs different kinds of operators. The results of their evaluation are also shown in comparison:

```
main()
{
int a, b, c, d;
a = 15; b = 10; c = ++a-b;
printf ("a = %d, b = %d, c = %d\n", a,b,c);
d=b++ + a;
printf ("a = %d, b = %d, d = %d\n, a,b,d);
printf ("a / b = %d\n, a / b);
printf ("a %% b = %d\n, a % b);
printf ("a *= b = %d\n, a *= b);
printf ("%d\n, (c > d) ? 1 : 0 );
printf ("%d\n, (c < d) ? 1 : 0 );
}
```

Notice the way the increment operator ++ works when used in an expression. In the statement c = ++a − b; new value a = 16 is used thus giving value 6 to C. That is, a is incremented by 1 before using in expression.

However in the statement d = b++ + a; The old value b = 10 is used in the expression. Here b is incremented after it is used in the expression.

We can print the character % by placing it immediately after another % character in the control string. This is illustrated by the statement.

printf("a %% b = %d\n", a%b);

This program also illustrates that the expression : c > d ? 1 : 0

Assumes the value 0 when c is less than d and 1 when c is greater than d.

Precedence in Arithmetic Operators:

An arithmetic expression without parenthesis will be evaluated from left to right using the rules of precedence of operators. There are two distinct priority levels of arithmetic operators in C.

High priority * / %
Low priority + -
Rules for evaluation of expression:

1. First parenthesized sub expression, left to right are evaluated.
2. If parentheses are nested, the evaluation begins with the innermost sub expression.
3. The precedence rule is applied in determining the order of application of operators in evaluating sub expressions.
4. The associability rule is applied when two or more operators of the same precedence level appear in the sub expression.
5. Arithmetic expressions are evaluated from left to right using the rules of precedence.
6. When Parenthesis is used, the expressions within parenthesis assume highest priority.

4.2. PRECEDENCE OF C OPERATORS

Operator precedence determines the grouping of terms in an expression. This affects how an expression is evaluated. Certain operators have higher precedence than others; for example, the multiplication operator has higher precedence than the addition operator:

Operators and Expressions

For example x = 7 + 3 * 2; Here x is assigned 13, not 20 because operator * has a higher precedence than + so it first gets multiplied with 3*2 and then adds 7.

Here operators with the highest precedence appear at the top of the table, and those with the lowest appear at the bottom.

Within an expression, higher precedence operators will be evaluated first.

Operator	Description	Associativity
() [] . -> ++ --	Parentheses (function call) (see Note 1) Brackets (array subscript) Member selection via object name Member selection via pointer Postfix increment/decrement (see Note 2)	left-to-right
++ -- + - ! ~ (type) * & sizeof	Prefix increment/decrement Unary plus/minus Logical negation/bitwise complement Cast (change type) Dereference Address Determine size in bytes	right-to-left
* / %	Multiplication/division/modulus	left-to-right
+ -	Addition/subtraction	left-to-right
<< >>	Bitwise shift left, Bitwise shift right	left-to-right
< <= > >=	Relational less than/less than or equal to Relational greater than/greater than or equal to	left-to-right
== !=	Relational is equal to/is not equal to	left-to-right
&	Bitwise AND	left-to-right
^	Bitwise exclusive OR	left-to-right
|	Bitwise inclusive OR	left-to-right
&&	Logical AND	left-to-right
||	Logical OR	left-to-right
?:	Ternary conditional	right-to-left
= += -= *= /= %= &= ^= |= <<= >>=	Assignment Addition/subtraction assignment Multiplication/division assignment Modulus/bitwise AND assignment Bitwise exclusive/inclusive OR assignment Bitwise shift left/right assignment	right-to-left
,	Comma (separate expressions)	left-to-right

Note 1:
Parentheses are also used to group sub-expressions to force a different precedence; such parenthetical expressions can be nested and are evaluated from inner to outer.

Note 2:
Postfix increment/decrement have high precedence, but the actual increment or decrement of the operand is delayed (to be accomplished sometime before the statement completes execution). So in the statement y = x * z++; the current value of z is used to evaluate the expression (i.e., z++ evaluates to z) and z only is incremented after all else is done.

```
Demo precedence of post-increment:
#include <stdio.h>
int main()
{
int i[] = {3, 5};
int *p = i;
int j = --*p++;
printf("j = %d\n\n", j);
system("pause");
return 0;
}
Output:
j=2
```

CONCLUDING REMARKS

You have now studied the various operators such as arithmetic, logical and relational, which are essential to write and execute programs. The precedence of the operators in the arithmetic operations is also furnished in the form of a table. The conditional, comma operators, and bitwise operators have been illustrated.

Chapter 5

PROGRAM CONTROL

ABSTRACT

This chapter deals with the loops that are used in the C programs. The scope of the loops such as for, while, and do-while are discussed. The technique of breaking the loop and continuing the same is also elaborated.

Outline:

- Conditional branching constructs
- Multi-level conditional branching constructs
- Looping Constructs

BRANCHING CONSTRUCTS

5.1. Conditional Branching Constructs

1. Simple If
2. If………….else
3. Else if Ladder
4. Nested If

Simple If:

The simplest form of the control statement is the If statement. It is very frequently used in decision making and allowing the flow of program execution.

The If structure has the following syntax:
if (condition)
statement;

The statement is any valid C language statement and the condition is any valid C language expression and frequently logical operators are used in the condition statement. The condition part should not end with a semicolon, since the condition and statement should be put together as a single statement. The command says if the conditions is true then perform the following statement and if the condition is fake the computer skips the statement and moves on to the next instruction in the program.

The above program checks the value of the input number to see if it is less than zero. If it is so then the following program statement which negates the value of the number is executed. If the value of the number is not less than zero, there is no need to negate it and the statement is automatically skipped. The absolute number is then displayed by the program, and program execution ends.

The If else construct:

The If else is actually just an extension of the general format of if statement. If the result of the condition is true, then program statement 1 is executed, otherwise program statement 2 will be executed. In any case either program statement 1 is executed or program statement 2 is executed but not both, when writing programs this else statement is so frequently required that almost all programming languages provide a special construct to handle this situation.

In the above program the If statement checks whether the given number is less than 0. If it is less than zero then it is negative and therefore the condition becomes true. The number that is negative is executed. If the number is not less than zero the If else construct skips the first statement and prints the second statement declaring that the number is positive.

Compound Relational tests:

C language provides the mechanisms necessary to perform compound relational tests. A compound relational test is simple one or more simple relational tests joined together by either the logical AND or the logical OR operators. These operators are represented by the character pairs && // respectively. The compound operators can be used to form complex expressions in C.

Syntax:

```
a> if (condition1 && condition2 && condition3)
b> if (condition1 || condition2 || condition3)
```

The syntax in the statement 'a' represents a complex if statement which combines different conditions using AND operator. In this case if only all the conditions are true then the whole statement is considered to be true. Even if one condition is false, the whole if statement is considered to be false.

The statement 'b' uses the logical operator or (||) to group different expression to be checked. In this case if any one of the expressions is found to be true, the whole expression is considered to be true. We can also use mixed expressions using logical operators and or together.

Nested if Statement:

The if statement may itself contain another if statement and this is known as nested if statement.

Syntax:

if (condition1)
 if (condition2)
 statement-1;
 else
 statement-2;
 else
 statement-3;

The if statement may be nested as deeply as you need to nest it. One block of code will only be executed if two conditions are true. Condition 1 is tested first and then condition 2 is tested. The second if condition is nested in the first. The second if condition is tested only when the first condition is true or else the program flow will skip to the corresponding else statement.

The ELSE If Ladder:

When a series of many conditions have to be checked we may use the ladder else if statement which takes the following general form.

if (condition1) statement – 1;
else if (condition2) statement2;
else if (condition3) statement3;
lse if (condition) statement n;

else default statement;
statement-x;

This construct is known as "if else construct or ladder". The conditions are evaluated from the top of the ladder down. As soon as the true condition is found, the statement associated with it is executed and the control is transferred to the statement – x (skipping the rest of the ladder. When all the conditions become false, the final else containing the default statement will be executed.

Example program using If else ladder to grade students according to the given rules:

Marks	Grade
70 to 100	DISTINCTION
60 to 69	IST CLASS
50 to 59	IIND CLASS
40 to 49	PASS CLASS
0 to 39	FAIL

5.2. Multi-Level Conditional Branching Constructs

The Switch Statement:

Unlike the If statement which allows a selection of two alternatives, the switch statement allows a program to select one statement for execution out of a set of alternatives. During the execution of the switch statement only one of the possible statements will be executed and the remaining statements will be skipped. The usage of multiple If else statement increases the complexity of the program since when the number of If else statements increase, it affects the readability of the program and makes it difficult to follow the program. The switch statement removes these disadvantages by using a simple and straight forward approach.

The general format of the Switch Statement is:

Switch (expression)
{
Case case-label-1;
Case case-label-2;
Case case-label-n;

....
Case default
}

When the switch statement is executed the control expression is evaluated first and the value is compared with the case label values in the given order. If the label matches with the value of the expression, then the control is transferred directly to the group of statements which follow the label. If none of the statements match, then the statement against the default is executed. The default statement is optional in switch statement in case if no default statement is given and if none of the conditions matches, then no action takes place and in such a case the control transfers to the next statement of the if else statement.

Un-Conditional Branching Constructs (or) Jump Statements:

Jump Statements

These statements transfer control to a different location within the code.

The GOTO statement:

The goto statement is a simple statement used to transfer the program control unconditionally from one statement to another statement. Although it might not be essential to use the goto statement in a highly structured language like C, there may be occasions when the use of goto is desirable.

Syntax:

goto label;
....
....
....
Label;
Statement;

The goto requires a label in order to identify the place where the branch is to be made. A label is a valid variable name followed by a colon.

The label is placed immediately before the statement where the control is to be transformed. A program may contain several goto statements that transferred to the same place in a program. The label must be unique. Control can be transferred out of or within a compound statement, and control can be transferred to the beginning of a compound statement. However the control cannot be transferred into a compound statement. The goto statement is discouraged in C, because it alters the sequential flow of logic that is the characteristic of C language.

5.3. Looping Constructs

Entry Control Looping:

1. for loop
2. while loop

Steps of Entry Control loops are as follows:

1. The test condition is evaluated and if it is true, the body of the loop is executed.
2. On execution of the body, text condition is repetitively checked and if it is true, the body is executed.
3. The process of execution of the body will continue till the test conditions become true.
4. The control is transferred out of the loop if test condition becomes false.

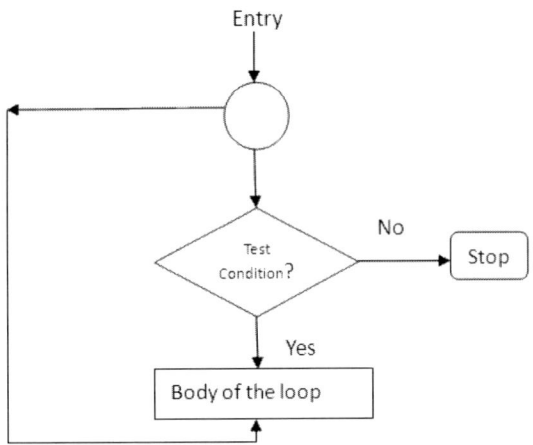

For Loop:
In for looping statement allows a number of lines to represent until the condition is satisfied.
Syntax:

for (initialize counter variable ; condition ; increment/decrement the counter variable)

{
Statement1;
...
Statement n;
}
WHILE LOOP:

In While looping statement allows a number of lines to represent until the condition is satisfied

Syntax:

while(condition)
{
Statement1;
...
Statement n;
}
Exit Control Looping:
do..while loop
for loop (also treated as exit control)

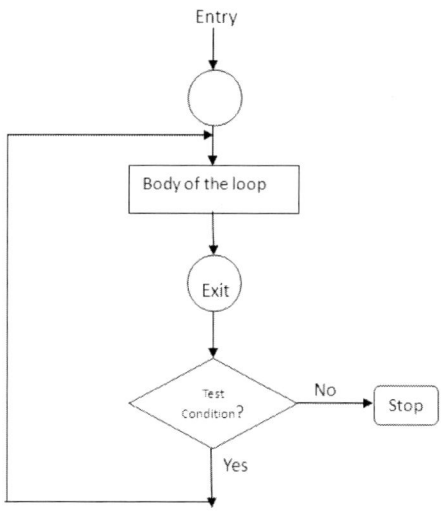

DO WHILE LOOP:

DO WHILE loop first executes the statements and then it checks the condition.

Syntax:
do
{
Statement1;
...
Statement n;
}while(condition);

Conclusion

In FOR LOOP:
No need to initialize variable before the loop

In WHILE LOOP:
To initialize the variable before the loop. Increment/decrement variable within the loop.

In DO WHILE LOOP:
Once it executes If the condition is TRUE/FALSE.

Break and continue statements:
C provides two commands to control how we loop:

1. break -- exit form loop or switch.
2. continue -- skip 1 iteration of loop.

Here is an example showing usage of *break* statement.

```
#include < stdio.h >
void main()
{
int I, num=0;
float sum=0,average;
printf("Input the marks, -1 to end\n");
while(1)
scanf("%d",&I); // read and store the input number
```

```
if(I==-1) // check whether input number is -1
break; //if number –1 is input skip the loop
sum+=I; //else add the value of I to sum
num++ // increment num value by 1
}
}
```

Here is an example showing usage of *continue* statement.

```
#include < stdio.h >
main()
{
int i;
int j = 10;
for( i = 0; i <= j; i ++ )
{
if( i == 5 )
{
continue;
}
printf("Hello %d\n", i );
}
}
```

This will produce the following output:

Hello 0
Hello 1
Hello 2
Hello 3
Hello 4
Hello 6
Hello 7
Hello 8
Hello 9
Hello 10

CONCLUDING REMARKS

The scope of the loops such as for loop, while loop, and do-while loop has been narrated in this chapter.

Chapter 6

STANDARD INPUT/OUTPUT

ABSTRACT

This chapter focuses on formatted functions such as printf() and scanf() statements. The unformatted functions such as putchar(), getche(), and gets() are also described with a few examples. The different data types and conversion symbols used in the C programs are elaborated.
Outline:

- Types of I/O Operations

MANAGING INPUT AND OUTPUT OPERATIONS

In this section you will learn about Single character input-output, String input and output, Formatted Input For scanf, Input specifications for real number, Input specifications for a character, Printing One Line, Conversion Strings, Specifiers, and Specifier Meaning.

6.1. TYPES OF I/O OPERATIONS

1. Formatted I/O operations
2. Unformatted I/O operations

Formatted Input For Scanf:

The formatted input refers to input data that has been arranged in a particular format. Input values are generally taken by using the scanf function. The scanf function has the general form,

scanf ("control string", arg1, arg2, arg3 ………….argn);

The format field is specified by the control string and the arguments are as given below. arg1, arg2, …………….argn specifies the address of location where address is to be stored. The control string specifies the field format which includes format specifications and optional number specifying field width and the conversion character % and also blanks, tabs and newlines. The Blanks, tabs and newlines are ignored by compiler. The conversion character % is followed by the type of data that is to be assigned to variables of the assignment. The field width specifier is optional. The general format for reading a integer number is

"% x d"

Here percent sign (%) denotes that a specifier for conversion follows and x is an integer number which specifies the width of the field of the number that is being read. The data type character d indicates that the number should be read in integer mode.

Example : scanf ("%3d %4d", &sum1, &sum2);

If the value inputs are 175 and 1342, value 175 is assigned to sum1 and value 1342 to sum 2. Suppose the input data was 1342 and 175. The number 134 will be assigned to sum1 and sum2 has the value 2 because of %3d the number 1342 will be cut to 134 and the remaining part is assigned to second variable sum2. If floating point numbers are assigned, then the decimal or fractional part is skipped by the computer. To read the long integer data type we can use conversion specifier % ld & % hd for short integer.

Unformatted console I/O functions.

The functions under this category are :

1. getch()
2. putch()
3. gets()
4. getche()

5. putchar()
6. puts()
7. getchar()
8. fputchar()
9. fgetchar()

These above listed functions broadly fall into two categories, the one which deals with a single character and the other which deals with a string of characters.

Explanations:

getch() : This function will read a single character the instant it is typed by the programmer without waiting for the Enter Key to be hit. The typed character is not echoed on screen.

getche() : This function will also read a single character the instant it is typed by the programmer without waiting for the Enter key to be hit, just like getch() function. The additional character 'e' in function getch() echoes the character on screen that was typed. This is the point of difference between getch() & getche().

getchar() : It works similar to that of getch() and also echoes the character typed on the screen but it requires enter key to be hit immediately after the character that was typed. It is a macro.

fgetchar() : It will echo the character on screen and it requires hit of Enter key immediately following the character. The only difference between getchar() and fgetchar() is that the former is a macro and latter is function.

putch() : It writes a character to the screen.

putchar() : It writes a character to the screen and is a macro.

fputchar() : It writes a character to the screen (function version).

(Note : putch(), putchar() and fputchar() can output only one character at a time on screen.)

gets() : It gets a string from the keyboard and it is necessary on the programmer's part to terminate that string with an Enter key. That's why spaces and tabs are acceptable as a part of the input string if gets() is used to read only one string at a time.

puts() : It outputs a string to the screen and puts() can output only one string at a time.

The above mentioned in-built functions have their own advantages and characteristics. Even though it has a number of the advantages, the mostly used functions are as follows:

1. getch()
2. getche()
3. gets()
4. pets()

CONCLUDING REMARKS

Formatted functions and unformatted functions have been illustrated with suitable examples.

Chapter 7

FUNCTIONS

ABSTRACT

This chapter introduces functions. Intialization of a functions, actual arguments, formal arguments, and return statement are described. Recursive functions are explained with examples.
Outline:

- Introduction
- Structure of a function
- Advantages of using functions
- Types of functions
- Nesting of functions
- Recursion

7.1. INTRODUCTION

A function in C language is a block of code that performs a specific task. It has a name and it is reusable i.e. it can be executed from as many different parts in a C Program as required. It also optionally returns a value to the calling program.

So function in a C program has some properties as discussed below.

1. Every function has a unique name. This name is used to call function from "main()" function. A function can be called from within another function.

2. A function is independent and it can perform its task without intervention from or interfering with other parts of the program.
3. A function performs a specific task. A task is a distinct job that your program must perform as a part of its overall operation, such as adding two or more integers, sorting an array into numerical order, or calculating a cube root etc.
4. A function returns a value to the calling program. This is optional and depends upon the task your function is going to accomplish. Suppose you want to just show few lines through function then it is not necessary to return a value. But if you are calculating area of a rectangle and wanted to use the result somewhere in the program, then you have to send back (return) value to the calling function.

C language is a collection of various inbuilt functions. If you have written a program in C then it is evident that you have used C's inbuilt functions. Printf(), scanf(), clrscr() etc. all are C's inbuilt functions. You cannot imagine a C program without function.

7.2. STRUCTURE OF A FUNCTION

A general form of a C function looks like this:
<return type> FunctionName (Argument1, Argument2, Argument3......)
{
Statement1;
Statement2;
Statement3;
}

An example of function.
int sum (int x, int y)
{
int result;
result = x + y;
return (result);
}

7.3. ADVANTAGES OF USING FUNCTIONS

There are many advantages in using functions in a program:

1. It makes possible top down modular programming. In this style of programming, the high level logic of the overall problem is solved first while the detail of each lower level function is addressed later.
2. The length of the source program can be reduced by using functions at appropriate places.
3. It becomes uncomplicated to locate and separate a faulty function for further study.
4. A function may be used later by many other programs which means that a c programmer can use the function written by others, instead of starting over from scratch.
5. A function can be used to keep away from rewriting the same block of codes which we are going use in two or more locations in a program. This is especially useful if the code involved is long or complicated.

7.4. TYPES OF FUNCTIONS

A function may belong to any one of the following categories:

1. Functions with no arguments and no return values.
2. Functions with arguments and no return values.
3. Functions with arguments and return values.
4. Functions that return multiple values. (with the help of pointers only)***
5. Functions with no arguments and return values.

Note that the *** can be used in most of the places since it uses the in-memory-place replacement techniques which reduces additional memory usage!

Functions and Variables:

Each function behaves the same way as the C language standard function *main()*. So a function will have its own local variables defined. In the above example *total* variable is local to the function Demo.

A global variable can be accessed in any function in similar way it is accessed in *main()* function.

Declaration and Definition:

When a function is defined at any place in the program, then it is called function definition. At the time of definition of a function actual logic is implemented with-in the function.

1. A function declaration does not have any body and they just have their interfaces.
2. A function declaration is usually declared at the top of a C source file, or in a separate header file.
3. A function declaration is sometimes called function prototype or function signature. For the above *Demo()* function which returns an integer and takes two parameters, a function declaration will be as follows:

int Demo(int par1, int par2);

Passing Parameters to a Function:
There are two ways to pass parameters to a function:

1. Pass by Value: This mechanism is used when you don't want to change the value of passed paramters. When parameters are passed by value then functions in C create copies of the passed in variables and do the required processing on these copied variables.
2. Pass by Reference: This mechanism is used when you want a function to do the changes in passed parameters and reflect those changes back to the calling function. In this case only addresses of the variables are passed to a function so that the function can work directly over the addresses.

Here are two programs to understand the differences.
Pass by value:

```
#include <stdio.h>
/* function declaration goes here.*/
void swap( int p1, int p2 );
int main()
{
int a = 10;
```

```
int b = 20;
printf("Before: Value of a = %d and value of b = %d\n", a, b );
swap( a, b );
printf("After: Value of a = %d and value of b = %d\n", a, b );
}
void swap( int p1, int p2 )
{
int t;
t = p2;
p2 = p1;
p1 = t;
printf("Value of a (p1) = %d and value of b(p2) = %d\n", p1, p2 );
}
```

Following is the result produced by the above example. Here the values of a and b remain unchanged before calling *swap* function and after calling *swap* function.

```
Before: Value of a = 10 and value of b = 20
Value of a (p1) = 20 and value of b(p2) = 10
After: Value of a = 10 and value of b = 20
```

Pass by reference:

```
#include <stdio.h>
/* function declaration goes here.*/
void swap( int *p1, int *p2 );
int main()
{
int a = 10;
int b = 20;
printf("Before: Value of a = %d and value of b = %d\n", a, b );
swap( &a, &b );
printf("After: Value of a = %d and value of b = %d\n", a, b );
}
void swap( int *p1, int *p2 )
{
int t;
t = *p2;
*p2 = *p1;
```

```
*p1 = t;
printf("Value of a (p1) = %d and value of b(p2) = %d\n", *p1, *p2 );
}
```

Here is the result produced by the above example. Here the values of a and b change after calling *swap* function.

Before: Value of a = 10 and value of b = 20
Value of a (p1) = 20 and value of b(p2) = 10
After: Value of a = 20 and value of b = 10

7.5. NESTING OF FUNCTIONS

C permits nesting of two functions freely. There is no limit as to how deeply functions can be nested. Suppose function a can call function b and function b can call function c and so on. Consider the following program:

```
main()
{
int a,b,c;
float ratio();
scanf("%d%d%d",&a,&b,&c);
printf("%fn",ratio(a,b,c));
}
float ratio(x,y,z)
int x,y,z;
{
if(difference(y,z))
return(x/y-z));
else
return(0,0);
}
difference(p,q)
{
int p,q;
{
if(p!=q)
return(1);
else
return(0);
```

}
The above program calculates the ratio a/b-c; and prints the result. We have the following three functions:

main()
ratio()
difference()

main reads the value of a,b,c and calls the function ratio to calculate the value a/b-c) this ratio cannot be evaluated if(b-c) is zero. Therefore ratio calls another function difference to test whether the difference (b-c) is zero or not.

7.6. RECURSION

Recursive function is a function that calls itself. When a function calls another function and that second function calls the third function, then this kind of a function is called nesting of functions. But a recursive function is the function that calls itself repeatedly.

A simple example:
main()
{
printf("this is an example of recursive function");
main();
}

when this program is executed, the line is printed repeatedly and indefinitely. We might have to abruptly terminate the execution.

```
int fact (int n)
{
if(n<0)              return -1;
if(n==0)             return 1;
else                 return (n*fact(n-1));
}
```

The scope and lifetime of variables in functions:

The scope and lifetime of the variables defined in C are not same when compared to other languages. The scope and lifetime depend on the storage class of the variable in c language. The variables can be any one of the four storage classes:

1. Automatic Variables
2. External variable
3. Static variable
4. Register variable.

The scope actually determines over which part or parts of the program the variable is available. The lifetime of the variable retains a given value during the execution of the program. Variables can also be categorized as local or global. Local variables are the variables that are declared within that function and are accessible to all the functions in a program and they can be declared within a function or outside the function also.

CONCLUDING REMARKS

You have studied how to initialize and use functions while writing programs in C. How the functions interact with one another is also explained with examples. The reader should know that the function always returns the integer value. The recursive nature of function has also been explained with suitable examples.

Chapter 8

STRINGS AND ARRAYS

ABSTRACT

This chapter deals with one, two and multi dimensional arrays with numerous programming examples. Array declaration and initialization are discussed.
Outline:

- What is an Array?
- Types of Arrays
- Declaration of Arrays

8.1. WHAT IS AN ARRAY?

An array in C language is a collection of similar data-types, which means that an array can hold value of a particular data type for which it has been declared. Arrays can be created from any of the C data-types int, float, and char. So an integer array can only hold integer values and cannot hold values other than integer. When we declare array, it allocates contiguous memory location for storing values whereas 2 or 3 variables of same data-type can have random locations. This is the most important difference between a variable and an array.

8.2. Types of Arrays

1) One dimension array (Also known as 1-D array).
2) Two dimension array (Also known as 2-D array).
3) Multi-dimension array.

8.3. Declaration of Arrays

Like any other variable, arrays must be declared before they are used. The general form of declaration is:

type variable-name[10];

The type specifies the type of the elements that will be contained in the array, such as int float or char and the size indicates the maximum number of elements that can be stored inside the array for ex:

int a[10];

a[0]	a[1]	a[2]	a[3]	a[4]	a[5]	a[6]	a[7]	a[8]	a[9]

Initialization of arrays:
We can initialize the elements in the array in the same way as the ordinary variables when they are declared. The general form of initialization off arrays is:

type array_name[size]={list of values};
The values in the list care separated by commas, for example the statement
int counter[]={1,1,1,1};

The initialization of arrays in c suffers two draw backs. They are as follows:

1. There is no convenient way to initialize only selected elements.
2. There is no shortcut method to initialize large number of elements.

/* Program to count the number of positive and negative numbers*/

```
#include< stdio.h >
void main( )
{
int a[50],n,count_neg=0,count_pos=0,I;
printf("Enter the size of the arrayn");
scanf("%d",&n);
printf("Enter the elements of the arrayn");
for I=0;I < n;I++)
scanf("%d",&a[I]);
for(I=0;I < n;I++)
{
if(a[I] < 0)
count_neg++;
else
count_pos++;
}
printf("There are %d negative numbers in the arrayn",count_neg);
printf("There are %d positive numbers in the arrayn",count_pos);
}
```

Multidimensional Arrays:

Often there is a need to store and manipulate two dimensional data structure such as matrices & tables. Here the array has two subscripts. One subscript denotes the row & the other the column.

The declaration of two dimension arrays is as follows:

data_type array_name[row_size][column_size];

int m[10][20]

Elements of multi dimension arrays:

A 2 dimensional array marks [4][3] is shown below. The first element is given by marks [0][0] and contains 35.5 & second element has marks [0][1] and contains 40.5 and so on.

marks [0][0] 35.5	Marks [0][1] 40.5	Marks [0][2] 45.5
marks [1][0] 50.5	Marks [1][1] 55.5	Marks [1][2] 60.5
marks [2][0]	Marks [2][1]	Marks [2][2]
marks [3][0]	Marks [3][1]	Marks [3][2]

Initialization of multidimensional arrays:

Like the one dimension arrays, 2 dimension arrays may be initialized by following their declaration with a list of initial values enclosed in braces

Example:

int table[2][3]={0,0,0,1,1,1};

Initializes the elements of first row to zero and second row to 1. The initialization is done row by row. The above statement can be equivalently written as

int table[2][3]={{0,0,0},{1,1,1}}

Handling of character string:

A string is a sequence of characters. Any sequence or set of characters defined within double quotation symbols is a constant string. In c it is required to do some meaningful operations on strings and they are:

- Reading string displaying strings
- Combining or concatenating strings
- Copying one string to another.
- Comparing strings & checking whether they are equal
- Extraction of a portion of a string

Strings are stored in memory as ASCII codes of characters that make up the string appended with '\0' (ASCII value of null). Normally each character is stored in one byte; successive characters are stored in successive bytes.

Character	m	Y		A	g	e		i	s
ASCII Code	77	121	32	97	103	10	32	105	115

The last character is the null character having ASCII value zero.

Character		2		(	t	w	o	)	\0
ASCII Code	32	50	32	40	116	119	41	0	0

Reading Strings from the terminal:

The function scanf with %s format specification is needed to read the character string from the terminal.

Example:

char address[15];

scanf("%s",address);

scanf statement has a drawback as it just terminates the statement as soon as it finds a blank space. Suppose if we type the string new York, then only the string 'new' will be read and since there is a blank space after word "new" it will terminate the string.

Note that we can use the scanf without the ampersand symbol before the variable name.

The function getchar can be used repeatedly to read a sequence of successive single characters and store it in the array.

We cannot manipulate strings since C does not provide any operators for strings. For instance we cannot assign one string to another directly.

For example:

String="xyz";

String1=string2;

are not valid. To copy the chars in one string to another string, we may only do so on a character to character basis.

Writing strings to screen:

The printf statement along with format specifier %s is used to print strings on to the screen. The format %s can be used to display an array of characters that is terminated by the null character. For example, printf("%s",name); can be used to display the entire contents of the array name.

Arithmetic operations on characters:

We can also manipulate the characters as we manipulate numbers in c language. Whenever the system encounters the character data, it is automatically converted into a integer value by the system. We can represent a character as an interface by using the following method.

x='a';

printf("%d\n",x);

Will display 97 on the screen. Arithmetic operations can also be performed on characters. For example, x='z'-1; is a valid statement. The

ASCII value of 'z' is 122 and the statement therefore will assign 121 to variable x.

It is also possible to use character constants in relational expressions for example

ch>'a' && ch <= 'z' will check whether the character stored in variable ch is a lower case letter. A character digit can also be converted into its equivalent integer value. Suppose the expression a=character-'1'; where a is defined as an integer variable & character contains value 8, then a= ASCII value of 8 ASCII value '1'=56-49=7.

We can also get the support of the c library function to convert a string of digits into their equivalent integer values. The general format of the function in x=atoi(string) here x is an integer variable & string is a character array containing string of digits.

CONCLUDING REMARKS

You have now learnt how to initialize an array in different ways. The characteristics of arrays have been discussed in depth. How to specify the elements of one-dimensional, two-dimensional and three or multidimensional are explained in detail together with examples.

Chapter 9

STRUCTURES, UNION, BIT FIELDS

ABSTRACT

This chapter explains the concept of structure. Various topics under structure such as declaration and initialization of structures, structure within structure, array of structure, and pointer to structure are elaborated.
Outline:

- Structures and Unions
- Declaring structure variable
- Structure within Structure
- Union within a Structure

9.1. STRUCTURES AND UNIONS

Let us look at Structures and Unions, Giving values to members, Initializing structure, Functions and structures, Passing structure to elements to functions, Passing entire function to functions, Arrays of structure, Structure within a structure and Union.

Arrays are used to store large sets of data and manipulate them but the disadvantage is that all the elements stored in an array are to be of the same data type. If we need to use a collection of different data type items it is not possible to use an array. When we require using a collection of different data items of different data types we can use a structure. A Structure is a method of packing data of different types. A structure is a convenient method of handling a group of related data items of different data types.

Structure Definition:
General format:
struct tag_name
{
data type member1;
data type member2;
...
...
}
Example:
struct lib_books
{
char title[20];
char author[15];
int pages;
float price;
};

The keyword struct declares a structure to hold the details of four fields namely title, author pages and price. These are members of the structures. Each member may belong to different or same data type. The tag name can be used to define objects that have the tag names structure. The structure we just declared is not a variable by itself but a template for the structure.

9.2. Declaring Structure Variable

We can declare structure variables using the tag name any where in the program. For example the statement,
struct lib_books book1,book2,book3;
declares book1,book2,book3 as variables of type struct lib_books and each declaration has four elements of the structure lib_books. The complete structure declaration might look like this

struct lib_books
{
char title[20];
char author[15];
int pages;

float price;
};
struct lib_books, book1, book2, book3;

structures do not occupy any memory until they are associated with the structure variable such as book1. the template is terminated with a semicolon. While the entire declaration is considered as a statement, each member is declared independently for its name and type in a separate statement inside the template. The tag name such as lib_books can be used to declare structure variables of its data type later in the program.

Giving values to members:

As mentioned earlier the members themselves are not variables and they should be linked to structure variables in order to make them meaningful members. The link between a member and a variable is established using the member operator '.' which is known as dot operator or period operator

For example:

Book1.price

is the variable representing the price of book1 and can be treated like any other ordinary variable. We can use scanf statement to assign values like

scanf("%s",book1.file);
scanf("%d",& book1.pages);
Or we can assign variables to the members of book1
strcpy(book1.title,"Medium-Advanced");
strcpy(book1.author,"Nandakumar");
book1.pages=250;
book1.price=28.50;

Initializing structure:

Like other data types we can initialize structures when we declare them. As for initalization goes, structure obeys the same set of rules as arrays. We initalize the fields of a structure by the following structure declaration with a list containing values for which fields as with arrays and these values must be evaluated at compile time.

Example:

Struct student newstudent
{
12345,

"kapildev"
"Pes college";
"Cse";
19;
};

this initializes the id_no field to 12345, the name field to "kapildev", the address field to "pes college", the field combination to "cse" and the age field to 19.

Functions and structures:

We can pass structures as arguments to functions. Unlike array names however, which always point to the start of the array, structure names are not pointers. As a result, when we change the structure parameter inside a function, we do not effect its corresponding argument.

Passing structure to elements to functions:

A structure may be passed into a function as individual member or a separate variable. A program example to display the contents of a structure passing the individual elements to a function is shown below.

```
# include <stdio.h>
void main()
{
int emp_id;
char name[25];
char department[10];
float salary;
};
static struct emp1={125,"sampath","operator",7500.00};
/* pass only emp_id and name to display function*/
display(emp1.emp_id,emp1.name);
}
/* function to display structure variables*/
display(e_no,e_name)
int e_no,e_name;
{
printf("%d%s",e_no,e_name);
```

in the declaration of structure type, emp_id and name have been declared as integer and character array. When we call the function display() using

Structures, Union, Bit Fields 59

display(emp1.emp_id,emp1.name); we are sending the emp_id and name to function display(0); it can be immediately realized that to pass individual elements would become more tedious as the number of structure elements go on increasing. A better way would be to pass the entire structure variable at a time.

Passing entire function to functions:

In the case of structures having numerous structure elements, passing these individual elements would be a tedious task. In such a case we may pass the whole structure to a function as shown below:

```
# include <stdio.h>
{
int emp_id;
char name[25];
char department[10];
float salary;
};
void main()
{
static struct employee emp1=
{
12,
"sadanand",
"computer",
7500.00
};
/*sending entire employee structure*/
display(emp1);
}
/*function to pass entire structure variable*/
display(empf)
struct employee empf
{
   printf("%d%s,%s,%f",
empf.empid,empf.name,empf.department,empf.salary);
}
```

Arrays of structure:

It is possible to define an array of structures. For example, if we are maintaining information about all the students in a college and if 100 students are studying in the college, we need to use an array rather than single variables. We can define an array of structures as shown in the following example:

```
structure information
{
int id_no;
char name[20];
char address[20];
char combination[3];
int age;
}
student[100];
```

An array of structures can be assigned initial values just as any other array. Remember that each element is a structure that must be assigned corresponding initial values as illustrated below.

```
#include <stdio.h>
{
struct info
{
int id_no;
char name[20];
char address[20];
char combination[3];
int age;
}
struct info std[100];
int I,n;
printf("Enter the number of students");
scanf("%d",&n);
printf(" Enter Id_no,name address combination agem");
for(I=0;I < n;I++)
    scanf(%d%s%s%s%d",&std[I].id_no,std[I].name,std[I].address,std[I].combination,&std[I].age);
    printf("n Student information");
```

```
for (I=0;I< n;I++)
printf("%d%s%s%s%dn",
",std[I].id_no,std[I].name,std[I].address,std[I].combination,std[I].age);
}
```

9.3. STRUCTURE WITHIN A STRUCTURE

A structure may be defined as a member of another structure. In such structures the declaration of the embedded structure must appear before the declaration of other structures.

```
struct date
{
int day;
int month;
int year;
};
struct student
{
int id_no;
char name[20];
char address[20];
char combination[3];
int age;
structure date def;
structure date doa;
}oldstudent, newstudent;
```

The structure student contains another structure date as its one of its members.

Union:

Unions like structures contain members whose individual data types may differ from one another. However all the members that compose a union share the same storage area within the computer's memory whereas each member within a structure is assigned its own unique storage area. Thus unions are used to conserve memory. They are useful for applications involving multiple members where values need not be assigned to all the members at any one time. Like structures, union can be declared using the keyword union as follows:

```
union item
{
int m;
float p;
char c;
}
code;
```

This declares a variable code of type union item. The union contains three members each with a different data type. However we can use only one of them at a time. This is because if only one location is allocated for union variable irrespective of size, the compiler allocates a piece of storage that is large enough to access a union member. We can use the same syntax that we use to access structure members. That is

```
code.m
code.p
code.c
```

are all valid member variables. During accessing we should make sure that we are accessing the member whose value is currently stored. For example a statement such as

```
code.m=456;
code.p=456.78;
printf("%d",code.m);
```

would produce erroneous result. In effect, a union creates a storage location that can be used by one of its members at a time. When a different number is assigned a new value the new value supercedes the previous member's value. Unions may be used in all places where a structure is allowed. The notation for accessing a union member that is nested inside a structure remains the same as for the nested structure.

typedef Keyword:

There is an easier way to define structs or you could "alias" types you create. For example:

```
typedef struct{
char firstName[20];
char lastName[20];
char SSN[10];
float gpa;
}student;
```

Now you can use *student* directly to define variables of *student* type without using struct keyword. Following is the example:

student student_a;

You can use typedef for non-structs:

```
typedef long int *pint32;
pint32 x, y, z;
```

x, y and z are all pointers to long int.

9.4. UNION WITHIN A STRUCTURE

```
#include <string.h>
#include <stdio.h>

typedef union {
 int units;
 float kgs;
 } amount ;

typedef struct {
 char selling[15];
 float unitprice;
 int unittype;
```

```
    amount howmuch;
} product;

int main()
    {
product dieselmotorbike;
product apples;
product * myebaystore[2];
int nitems = 2; int i;

strcpy(dieselmotorbike.selling,"A Diesel Motor Cycle");
dieselmotorbike.unitprice = 5488.00;
dieselmotorbike.unittype = 1;
dieselmotorbike.howmuch.units = 4;

strcpy(apples.selling,"Granny duBois");
apples.unitprice = 0.78;
apples.unittype = 2;
apples.howmuch.kgs = 0.5;

myebaystore[0] = &dieselmotorbike;
myebaystore[1] = &apples;

for (i=0; i<nitems; i++) {
printf("\n%s\n",myebaystore[i]->selling);
switch (myebaystore[i]->unittype) {
case 1:
printf("We have %d units for sale\n",
myebaystore[i]->howmuch.units);
break;
case 2:
printf("We have %f kgs for sale\n",
myebaystore[i]->howmuch.kgs);
break;
        }
    }
}
```

Conclusion:

1. You can create arrays of structs.
2. Structs can be copied or assigned.
3. The & operator may be used with structs to show addresses.
4. Structs can be passed into functions. Structs can also be returned from functions.
5. Structs cannot be compared!
6. Structures can store non-homogenous data types into a single collection, much like an array does for common data (except it isn't accessed in the same manner).
7. Pointers to structs have a special infix operator: -> for dereferencing the pointer.
8. typedef can help you clear your code up and can help save some keystrokes

CONCLUDING REMARKS

One of the powerful features of C language is that it supports the creation of structure. For the beginners, the concepts and examples on structures are given in an easy way and a step by step process is adopted. The typedef facility can be used to create user-defined data types and is illustrated with many examples.

Chapter 10

POINTERS

ABSTRACT

In this chapter, you will learn about C Programming - Pointers, Pointer declaration, Address operator, Pointer expressions & pointer arithmetic, Pointers and function, Call by value, Call by Reference, Pointer to arrays, Pointers and structures, Pointers on pointer.
Outline:

- Introduction
- Pointer Declaration

10.1. INTRODUCTION

In c a pointer is a variable that points to or references a memory location in which data is stored. Each memory cell in the computer has an address that can be used to access that location so a pointer variable points to a memory location we can access and change the contents of this memory location via the pointer.

10.2. POINTER DECLARATION

type * variable name

Example:

int *ptr;
float *string;

Reference operator (&):
As soon as we declare a variable, the amount of memory needed is assigned for it at a specific location in memory (its memory address). We generally do not actively decide the exact location of the variable within the panel of cells that we have imagined the memory to be - Fortunately, that is a task automatically performed by the operating system during runtime. However, in some cases we may be interested in knowing the address where our variable is being stored during runtime in order to operate with relative positions to it.

The address that locates a variable within memory is what we call a reference to that variable. This reference to a variable can be obtained by preceding the identifier of a variable with an ampersand sign (&), known as reference operator, which can be literally translated as "address of".

This would assign to ted the address of variable and y, since when preceding the name of the variable andy with the reference operator (&) we are no longer talking about the content of the variable itself, but about its reference (i.e., its address in memory).

From now on we are going to assume that andy is placed during runtime in the memory address 1776. This number (1776) is just an arbitrary assumption we are inventing right now in order to help clarify some concepts in this tutorial, but in reality, we cannot know before runtime the real value the address of a variable will have in memory. Consider the following code fragment:

1. andy = 25;
2. fred = andy;
3. ted = &andy;

The values contained in each variable after the execution of this, are shown in the following diagram:

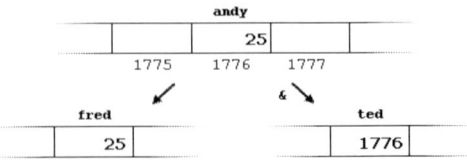

First, we have assigned the value 25 to andy (a variable whose address in memory we have assumed to be 1776).The second statement copied to fred the content of variable andy (which is 25). This is a standard assignment operation, as we have done so many times before. Finally, the third statement copies to ted not the value contained in andy but a reference to it (i.e., its address, which we have assumed to be 1776). The reason is that in this third assignment operation we have preceded the identifier andy with the reference operator (&), so we were no longer referring to the value of andy but to its reference (its address in memory).

The variable that stores the reference to another variable (like ted in the previous example) is what we call a pointer. Pointers are a very powerful feature of the C++ language that has many uses in advanced programming. Farther ahead, we will see how this type of variable is used and declared.

Dereference operator (*):

We have just seen that a variable which stores a reference to another variable is called a pointer. Pointers are said to "point to" the variable whose reference they store. Using a pointer we can directly access the value stored in the variable which it points to. To do this, we simply have to precede the pointer's identifier with an asterisk (*), which acts as dereference operator and that can be literally translated to "value pointed by". Therefore, following with the values of the previous example, if we write:

beth = *ted;

(that we could read as: "beth equal to value pointed by ted") beth would take the value 25, since ted is 1776, and the value pointed by 1776 is 25.

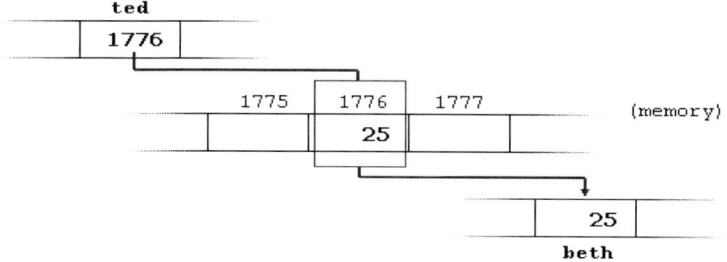

It must clearly be differentiated that the expression ted refers to the value 1776, while *ted (with an asterisk * preceding the identifier) refers to the value stored at address 1776, which in this case is 25. Notice the difference of including or not including the dereference operator (An explanatory commentary has to be included as to how each of these two expressions could be read):

beth = ted; // beth equal to ted (1776)
beth = *ted; // beth equal to value pointed by ted (25)

Notice the difference between the reference and dereference operators:

1. & is the reference operator and can be read as "address of"
2. is the dereference operator and can be read as "value pointed by"

Thus, they have complementary (or opposite) meanings. A variable referenced with & can be dereferenced with *. Earlier we performed the following two assignment operations:

andy = 25;
ted = &andy;

Right after these two statements, all of the following expressions would give true as result:

andy == 25
&andy == 1776
ted == 1776
*ted == 25

The first expression is quite clear considering that the assignment operation performed on andy was andy=25. The second one uses the reference operator (&), which returns the address of variable andy, which was assumed to have a value of 1776. The third one is somewhat obvious since the second expression was true and the assignment operation performed on ted was ted=&andy. The fourth expression uses the dereference operator (*) that, as seen, can be read as "value pointed by", and the value pointed by ted is indeed 25. So, after all that, it may also be infered that for as long as the address pointed by ted remains unchanged the following expression will also be true:

*ted == andy

Pointer expressions & pointer arithmetic:

Like other variables, pointer variables can be used in expressions. For example if p1 and p2 are properly declared and initialized pointers, then the following statements are valid.

y=*p1**p2;
sum=sum+*p1;
z= 5* - *p2/p1;
*p2= *p2 + 10;

C allows us to add integers to or subtract integers from pointers as well as to subtract one pointer from the other. We can also use short hand operators with the pointers p1+=; sum+=*p2; etc., we can also compare pointers by using relational operators and the expressions such as p1 >p2 , p1==p2 and p1!=p2 are allowed.

```
/*Program to illustrate the pointer expression and pointer arithmetic*/
#include< stdio.h >
main()
{
int ptr1,ptr2;
int a,b,x,y,z;
a=30;b=6;
ptr1=&a;
ptr2=&b;
x=*ptr1+ *ptr2 –6;
y=6*- *ptr1/ *ptr2 +30;
printf("\nAddress of a +%u",ptr1);
printf("\nAddress of b %u",ptr2);
printf("\na=%d, b=%d",a,b);
printf("\nx=%d,y=%d",x,y);
ptr1=ptr1 + 70;
ptr2= ptr2;
printf("\na=%d, b=%d",a,b);
}
```

Pointers and function:

The pointers are very much used in a function declaration. Sometimes only with a pointer can a complex function be easily represented with success. The usage of pointers in a function definition may be classified into two groups.

1. Call by reference
2. Call by value.

Call by value:

We have seen that when a function is invoked there will be a link established between the formal and actual parameters. A temporary storage is created where the value of actual parameters is stored. The formal parameter picks up its value from storage area and the mechanism of data transfer between actual and formal parameters allows the actual parameters the mechanism of data transfer which is referred as "call by value". The corresponding formal parameter represents a local variable in the called function. The current value of corresponding actual parameter becomes the initial value of formal parameter. The value of formal parameter may be changed in the body of the actual parameter. The value of formal parameter may be changed in the body of the subprogram by assignment or input statements. This will not change the value of actual parameters.

```
/* Include< stdio.h >
void main()
{
int x,y;
x=20;
y=30;
printf("\n Value of a and b before function call =%d %d",a,b);
fncn(x,y);
printf("\n Value of a and b after function call =%d %d",a,b);
}
fncn(p,q)
int p,q;
{
p=p+p;
```

q=q+q;
}

Call by Reference:

When we pass address to a function the parameters receiving the address should be pointers. The process of calling a function by using pointers to pass the address of the variable is known as "call by reference". The function which is called by reference can change the values of the variable used in the call.

```
/* example of call by reference*/
/* Include< stdio.h >
void main()
{
int x,y;
x=20;
y=30;
printf("\n Value of a and b before function call =%d %d",a,b);
fncn(&x,&y);
printf("\n Value of a and b after function call =%d %d",a,b);
}

fncn(p,q)
int p,q;
{
*p=*p+*p;
*q=*q+*q;
}
```

Pointer to arrays:

An array is actually very much like a pointer. We can declare the array's first element as a[0] or as int *a because a[0] is an address and *a is also an address and the form of declaration is equivalent. The difference is that pointer is a variable and can appear on the left of the assignment operator that is lvalue. The array name is constant and cannot appear on the left side of assignment operator.

/* A program to display the contents of array using pointer*/
main()

```
{
int a[100];
int i,j,n;
printf("\nEnter the elements of the array\n");
scanf("%d",&n);
printf("Enter the array elements");
for(I=0;I< n;I++)
scanf("%d",&a[I]);
printf("Array element are");
for(ptr=a,ptr< (a+n);ptr++)
printf("Value of a[%d]=%d stored at address %u",j+=,*ptr,ptr);
}
```

Strings are character arrays and here the last element is \0 arrays and pointers to char arrays can be used to perform a number of string functions.

Pointers and structures:

We know that the name of an array stands for the address of its zeroth element and the same concept applies for names of arrays of structures. Suppose item is an array variable of struct type, consider the following declaration:

```
struct products
{
char name[30];
int manufac;
float net;
}item[2],*ptr;
```

this statement declares item as array of two elements, each type struct products and ptr as a pointer data objects of type struct products, the

assignment ptr=item;

would assign the address of zeroth element to product[0]. Its members can be accessed by using the following notation.

ptr- >name;
ptr- >manufac;
ptr- >net;

The symbol - > is called arrow pointer and is made up of minus sign and greater than sign. Note that ptr- > is simple another way of writing product[0]. When the pointer is incremented by one it is made to pint to next record ie item[1]. The following statement will print the values of members of all the elements of the product array.

for(ptr=item; ptr< item+2;ptr++)
printf("%s%d%f\n",ptr- >name,ptr- >manufac,ptr- >net);

We could also use the notation (*ptr).number to access the member number. The parenthesis around ptr is necessary because the member operator '.' has a higher precedence than the operator *.

Pointers to pointer:

C++ allows the use of pointers that point to pointers, that these, in their turn, point to data (or even to other pointers). In order to do that, we only need to add an asterisk (*) for each level of reference in their declarations:

char a;
char * b;
char ** c;
a = 'z';
b = &a;
c = &b;

This, supposing the randomly chosen memory locations for each variable of 7230, 8092 and 10502, could be represented as:

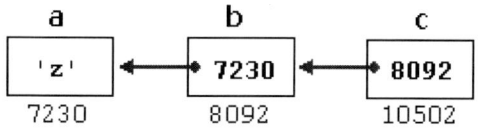

The value of each variable is written inside each cell; under the cells are their respective addresses in memory.

The new thing in this example is variable c, which can be used in three different levels of indirection, each one of them would correspond to a different value:

c has type char** and a value of 8092
c has type char and a value of 7230
**c has type char and a value of 'z'

The declaration of a pointer-to-pointer looks like : int **ipp;
where the two asterisks indicate that two levels of pointers are involved. Starting off with the familiar, uninspiring, kindergarten-style examples, we can demonstrate the use of ipp by declaring some pointers for it to point to and some ints for those pointers to point to:

int i = 5, j = 6; k = 7;
int *ip1 = &i, *ip2 = &j;

Now we can set ipp = &ip1; and ipp points to ip1 which points to i. *ipp is ip1, and **ipp is i, or 5. We can illustrate the situation, with our familiar box-and-arrow notation, like this:

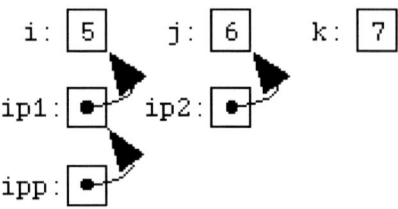

If we say *ipp = ip2;
we've changed the pointer pointed to by ipp (that is, ip1) to contain a copy of ip2, so that it (ip1) now points at j:

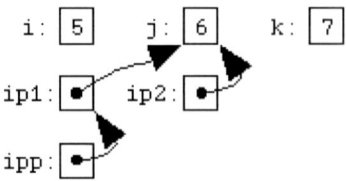

If we say   *ipp = &k;   we've changed the pointer pointed to by ipp (that is, ip1 again) to point to k:

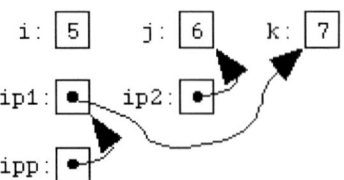

What are pointers to pointers good for, in practice? One use is returning pointers from functions, via pointer arguments rather than as the formal return value. To explain this, let's first step back and consider the case of returning a simple type, such as int, from a function via a pointer argument.

Example:
```
void func(int** pInt);
int main()
{
int nvar=2;
int* pvar=&nvar;
func(&pvar);
....
return 0;
}
void func(int** ppInt)
{
//Modify the pointer, ppInt points to
*ppInt=&g_One;
//You can also allocate memory, depending on your requirements
*ppInt=new int;

//Modify the variable, *ppInt points to
**ppInt=3;
}
```

Generic Pointers: (void Pointers):

The void type of pointer is a special type of pointer. In C++, void represents the absence of type, so void pointers are pointers that point to a value that has no type (and thus also an undetermined length and undetermined dereference properties). Let's see some of the things.

This allows void pointers to point to any data type, from an integer value or a float to a string of characters. But in exchange they have a great limitation: the data pointed by them cannot be directly dereferenced (which is logical, since we have no type to dereference to), and for that reason we will always have to cast the address in the void pointer to some other pointer type that points to a concrete data type before dereferencing it.

One of its uses may be to pass generic parameters to a function:

```
#include <iostream>
using namespace std;
```

```
void increase (void* data, int psize)
{
if ( psize == sizeof(char) )
{ char* pchar; pchar=(char*)data; ++(*pchar); }
else if (psize == sizeof(int) )
{ int* pint; pint=(int*)data; ++(*pint); }
}
int main ()
{
char a = 'x';
int b = 1602;
increase (&a,sizeof(a));
increase (&b,sizeof(b));
cout << a << ", " << b << endl;
return 0;
}
```

sizeof is an operator integrated in the C++ language that returns the size in bytes of its parameter. For non-dynamic data types this value is a constant. Therefore, for example, sizeof(char) is 1, because char type is one byte long.

Try the following code to understand Generic Pointers.

```
#include <stdio.h>
int main()
{
int i;
char c;
void *the_data;
i = 6;
c = 'a';
the_data = &i;
printf("the_data points to the integer value %d\n",
*(int*) the_data);
the_data = &c;
printf("the_data now points to the character %c\n",
*(char*) the_data);
return 0;
}
```

NOTE-1 : Here in the first print statement, the_data is prefixed by *(int*). This is called type casting in C language. Type is used to caste a variable from one data type to another datatype to make it compatible to the lvalue.

NOTE-2 : lvalue is something which is used to the left side of a statement and in which we can assign some value. A constant can't be an lvalue because we can not assign any value in contact. For example x = y, here x is lvalue and y is rvalue.

However, the above example will produce the following result:

the_data points to the integer value 6
the_data now points to the character a

Null pointer:
A null pointer is a regular pointer of any pointer type which has a special value that indicates that it is not pointing to any valid reference or memory address. This value is the result of type-casting the integer value zero to any pointer type.

int * p;
p = 0; // p has a null pointer value

Do not confuse null pointers with void pointers. A null pointer is a value that any pointer may take to represent that it is pointing to "nowhere", while a void pointer is a special type of pointer that can point to somewhere without a specific type. One refers to the value stored in the pointer itself and the other to the type of data it points to.

Pointers and const Type Qualifier:
The const type qualifier can make things a little confusing when it is used with pointer declarations.
Consider the below example:

const int * const ip; /* The pointer *ip is const and it points at is also cont */
int * const ip; /* The pointer *ip is const */
const int * ip; /* What *ip is pointing at is const */
int * ip; /* Nothing is const */

As can be seen, care must be taken when specifying the const qualifier using pointers.

Modifying Variables Using Pointers:

You know how to access the value pointed to using the dereference operator, but you can also modify the content of variables. To achieve this, put the dereferenced pointer on the left of the assignment operator, as shown in this example, which uses an array:

```
#include <stdio.h>
int main() {
char *ptr;
char arrayChars[8] = {'F','r','i','e','n','d','s','\0'};
ptr = arrayChars;
printf("The array reads %s.\n", arrayChars);
printf("Let's change it..... ");
*ptr = 'f'; /* ptr points to the first element */
printf(" now it reads %s.\n", arrayChars);
printf("The 3rd character of the array is %c.\n",
*(ptr+=2));
printf("Let's change it again..... ");
*(ptr - 1) = ' ';
printf("Now it reads %s.\n", arrayChars);
return 0;
}
```

This will produce the following result:
The array reads Friends.
Let's change it..... now it reads friends.
The 3rd character of the array is i.
Let's change it again..... Now it reads f iends.

Let us clarify one thing in this following question.:-

Between the int pointer and long double pointer which pointer will consume more memory space?

Answer: Size of any type of pointer is independent of the data type which it is pointing to i.e. size of the pointer is always fixed. Size of any type (near) of pointer in c is two bytes. Mostly all the pointers in the 4GB address space system architecture will occuy 2 Bytes. For example:

```
#include<stdio.h>
void main(){
```

int *p1;
long double *p2;
printf("%d %d",sizeof(p1),sizeof(p2));
}
Output: 2 2

Both pointers int and long double are pointing to first byte of int data and long double data respectively.

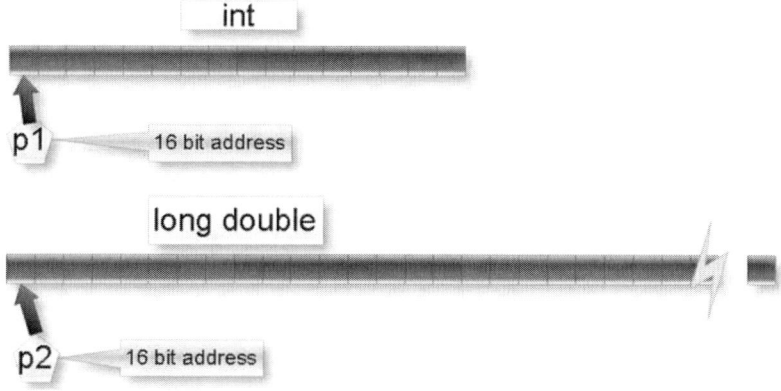

Hence both int pointer and long double pointer stores only address in 16 bits. Thus both of them will occupy exactly equal memory space.

What is the size of void pointer in c?

Answer:Size of any type of pointer in c is independent of the data type which the pointer is pointing i.e. the size of all types of pointers (near) in c is two byte whether it is char pointer, double pointer, function pointer or null pointer. Void pointer is not an exception to this rule and the size of void pointer is also two bytes.

Constant Pointers and Pointers to Constants:

Pointer contants and contant pointers are something that many people simply don't use. If you have a value in your program and it should not change, or if you have a pointer and you don't want it to be pointed to a different value, you should make it a constant with the const keyword. There are generally two places that the const keyword can be used when declaring a pointer. Consider the following declaration: char A_char = 'A';

char * myPtr = &A_char;

This is a simple declaration of the variable myPtr. myPtr is a pointer to a character variable and in this case points to the character 'A'. Don't be confused about the fact that a character pointer is being used to point to a single character—this is perfectly legal! Not every character pointer has to point to a string. Now consider the following three declarations assuming that char_A has been defined as a type char variable:

```
const char * myPtr = &char_A;
char * const myPtr = &char_A;
const char * const myPtr = &char_A;
```

What is the difference between each of the valid ones?

All the three are valid and correct declarations. Each assigns the addres of char_A to a character pointer. The difference is in what is constant.

The first declaration:

const char * myPtr

declares a pointer to a constant character. This pointer can not be used to change the value being pointed to:

```
char char_A = 'A';
const char * myPtr = &char_A;
*myPtr = 'J'; // error - can't change value of *myPtr
```

The second declaration:

char * const myPtr

declares a constant pointer to a character. The location stored in the pointer cannot change. You cannot change where this pointer points:

```
char char_A = 'A';
char char_B = 'B';
char * const myPtr = &char_A;
myPtr = &char_B; // error - can't change address of myPtr
```

The third declares a pointer to a character where both the pointer value and the value being pointed at will not change.

```
//POINTER TO CONSTANT vs CONSTANT POINTER:
#include<iostream.h>
#include<conio.h>
//POINTER TO CONSTANT
void f1()
{
int i=10,j=20;
```

```
const int* pi=&i;
cout<<*pi<<endl;
//*pi = 200; ERROR : CANNOT MODIFY A CONST OBJECT IN f1()
pi=&j; // IT CAN POINT ANOTHER CONSTANT
cout<<*pi<<endl;
}
//CONSTANT POINTER
void f2()
{
int i=100,j;
int* const pi=&i;
cout<<*pi<<endl;
*pi = 200; // IT CAN ASSIGN ANOTHER VALUE AT THIS ADDRESS
cout<<*pi<<endl;
//pi=&j; ERROR : CANNOT MODIFY A CONST OBJECT IN f2()
}
void main()
{
clrscr();
f1();
f2();
getch();
}
```

CONCLUDING REMARKS

This chapter describes the most important feature of C language i.e. pointer. The reader is made to understand clearly about the declaration and initialization of pointers and how to access variables using their pointers.

Chapter 11

FILE INPUT/OUTPUT

ABSTRACT

This chapter explains the procedure for opening files and storing information in them. The various I/O functions related to high level and low level file disk operations are elaborated with programming examples.
Outline:
- What is a file?
- File management in C
- File operation function in C

11.1. WHAT IS A FILE?

Abstractly, a file is a collection of bytes stored on a secondary storage device, which is generally a disk of some kind. The collection of bytes may be interpreted, for example, as characters, words, lines, paragraphs and pages from a textual document; fields and records belonging to a database; or pixels from a graphical image. The meaning attached to a particular file is determined entirely by the data structures and operations used by a program to process the file. It is conceivable (and it sometimes happens) that a graphics file will be read and displayed by a program designed to process textual data. The result is that no meaningful output probably occurs and this is to be expected. A file is simply a machine decipherable storage media where programs and data are stored for machine usage.

Essentially there are two kinds of files that programmers deal with-text files and binary files. These two classes of files are discussed in the following sections.

Binary files:

A binary file is not different from a text file. It is a collection of bytes. In C Programming Language a byte and a character are equivalent. Hence a binary file is also referred to as a character stream, but there are two essential differences.

No special processing of the data occurs and each byte of data is transferred to or from the disk unprocessed.

C Programming Language places no constructs on the file, and it may be read from, or written to, in any manner chosen by the programmer.

Binary files can be either processed sequentially or, depending on the needs of the application, can be processed using random access techniques. In C Programming Language, processing a file using random access techniques involves moving the current file position to an appropriate place in the file before reading or writing data. This indicates a second characteristic of binary files, which is they are a generally processed using read and write operations simultaneously.

11.2. FILE MANAGEMENT IN C

This deals with File management in C, File operation functions in C, Defining and opening a file, Closing a file, The getw and putw functions, The fprintf & fscanf functions, Random access to files and fseek function. C supports a number of functions that have the ability to perform basic file operations, which include:

1. Naming a file
2. Opening a file
3. Reading from a file
4. Writing data into a file
5. Closing a file

Real life situations involve large volume of data and in such cases, the console oriented I/O operations pose two major problems:

It becomes cumbersome and time consuming to handle large volumes of data through terminals.

File Input/Output

The entire data is lost when either the program is terminated or computer is turned off and therefore it is necessary to have a more flexible approach where data can be stored on the disks and read whenever necessary, without destroying the data. This method employs the concept of files to store data.

11.3. FILE OPERATION FUNCTIONS IN C

Function Name	Operation
fopen()	Creates a new file for use
	Opens a new existing file for use
Fclose()	Closes a file which has been opened for use
getc()	Reads a character from a file
putc()	Writes a character to a file
fprintf()	Writes a set of data values to a file
fscanf()	Reads a set of data values from a file
getw()	Reads a integer from a file
putw()	Writes an integer to the file
fseek()	Sets the position to a desired point in the file
ftell()	Gives the current position in the file
rewind()	Sets the position to the beginning of the file

Defining and opening a file:

If we want to store data in a file into the secondary memory, we must specify certain things about the file to the operating system. This may include the filename, data structure, and purpose. The general format of the function used for opening a file is

FILE *fp;
fp=fopen("filename","mode");

The first statement declares the variable fp as a pointer to the data type FILE. As stated earlier, File is a structure that is defined in the I/O Library. The second statement opens the file named filename and assigns an identifier to the FILE type pointer fp. This pointer, which contains all the information about the file, is subsequently used as a communication link between the system and the program.

The second statement also specifies the purpose of opening the file. The mode does this job.

R	Open for reading
r+	Open for reading and writing
W	Open for writing and create the file if it does not exist. If the file exists then make it blank.
w+	Open for reading and writing and create the file if it does not exist. If the file exists then make it blank.
A	Open for appending (writing at the end of file) and create the file if it does not exist.
a+	Open for reading and appending and create the file if it does not exist.

Consider the following statements:
FILE *p1, *p2;
p1=fopen("data","r");
p2=fopen("results","w");

In these statements the p1 and p2 are created and assigned to open the file data and results respectively. The file data is opened for reading and result is opened for writing. In case the results file already exists, its contents are deleted and the files are opened as a new file. If data file does not exist error will occur.

Closing a file:

The input output library supports the function to close a file; it is in the following format.

fclose(file_pointer);

A file must be closed as soon as all operations on it have been completed. This would close the file associated with the file pointer.

Observe the following program.

....
FILE *p1 *p2;
p1=fopen ("Input","w");
p2=fopen ("Output","r");
....
...
fclose(p1);
fclose(p2)

The above program opens two files and closes them after all operations on them are completed and once a file is closed its file pointer can be reversed on other file. The getc and putc functions are analogous to getchar and putchar functions and handle one character at a time. The putc function writes the character contained in character variable c to the file associated with the pointer fp1. ex putc(c,fp1); similarly getc function is used to read a character from a file that has been open in read mode. c=getc(fp2).

The program shown below displays use of a file operation. The data is entered through the keyboard and the program writes it character by character, to the file input. The end of the data is indicated by entering an EOF character, which is control-z. The file input is closed at this signal.

```
#include< stdio.h >
main()
{
file *f1;
printf("Data input output");
f1=fopen("Input","w"); /*Open the file Input*/
while((c=getchar())!=EOF) /*get a character from key board*/
putc(c,f1); /*write a character to input*/
fclose(f1); /*close the file input*/
printf("nData outputn");
f1=fopen("INPUT","r"); /*Reopen the file input*/
while((c=getc(f1))!=EOF)
printf("%c",c);
fclose(f1);
}
```

The getw and putw functions:

These are integer-oriented functions. They are similar to get c and putc functions and are used to read and write integer values. These functions would be useful when we deal with only integer data. The general forms of getw and putw are:

putw(integer,fp);
getw(fp);

```
/*Example program for using getw and putw functions*/
#include< stdio.h >
main()
{
FILE *f1,*f2,*f3;
int number I;
printf("Contents of the data filenn");
```

```
f1=fopen("DATA","W");
for(I=1;I< 30;I++)
{
scanf("%d",&number);
if(number==-1)
break;
putw(number,f1);
}
fclose(f1);
f1=fopen("DATA","r");
f2=fopen("ODD","w");
f3=fopen("EVEN","w");
while((number=getw(f1))!=EOF)/* Read from data file*/
{
if(number%2==0)
putw(number,f3);/*Write to even file*/
else
putw(number,f2);/*write to odd file*/
}
fclose(f1);
fclose(f2);
fclose(f3);
f2=fopen("ODD","r");
f3=fopen("EVEN","r");
printf("nnContents of the odd filenn");
while(number=getw(f2))!=EOF)
printf("%d%d",number);
printf("nnContents of the even file");
while(number=getw(f3))!=EOF)
printf("%d",number);
fclose(f2);
fclose(f3);
}
```

The fprintf & fscanf functions:

The fprintf and fscanf functions are identical to printf and scanf functions except that they work on files. The first argument of these functions is a file pointer which specifies the file to be used. The general form of fprintf is

fprintf(fp,"control string", list);

File Input/Output

Where fp id is a file pointer associated with a file that has been opened for writing. The control string is file output specifications list which may include variable, constant and string.

fprintf(f1,%s%d%f",name,age,7.5);

Here name is an array variable of type char and age is an int variable. The general format of fscanf is

fscanf(fp,"controlstring",list);

This statement would cause the reading of items in the control string.
Example:
fscanf(f2,"5s%d",item,&quantity");

Like scanf, fscanf also returns the number of items that are successfully read.

```
/*Program to handle mixed data types*/
#include< stdio.h >
main()
{
FILE *fp;
int num,qty,I;
float price,value;
char item[10],filename[10];
printf("Input filename");
scanf("%s",filename);
fp=fopen(filename,"w");
printf("Input inventory datann"0;
printf("Item namem number price quantityn");
for I=1;I< =3;I++)
{
fscanf(stdin,"%s%d%f%d",item,&number,&price,&quality);
fprintf(fp,"%s%d%f%d",itemnumber,price,quality);
}
fclose (fp);
fprintf(stdout,"nn");
fp=fopen(filename,"r");
printf("Item name number price quantity value");
for(I=1;I< =3;I++)
{
fscanf(fp,"%s%d%f%d",item,&number,&prince,&quality);
value=price*quantity");
fprintf("stdout,"%s%d%f%d%dn",item,number,price,quantity,value);
```

}
fclose(fp);
}

Data files using structures:

You can read and write structures to data files in the same way as you do with any other data type. Here is an example:

```
#include<stdio.h>
Struct
{
char name[100];
    int age;
} p;
int main()
{
FILE *f;
    strcpy(p.name,"John");
    p.age = 25;
    f = fopen("test.dat","wb");
    fwrite(&p,1,sizeof(p),f);
fclose(f);
    return 0;
}
```

Sequential and Random Access File Handling in C:

In computer programming, the two main types of file handling are:

Sequential

Random access.

Sequential files are generally used in cases where the program processes the data in a sequential fashion – i.e. counting words in a text file – although in some cases, random access can be feigned by moving backwards and forwards over a sequential file.

True random access file handling, however, only accesses the file at the point at which the data should be read or written, rather than having to process it sequentially. A hybrid approach is also possible whereby a part of the file is used for sequential access to locate something in the random access portion of the file, in much the same way that a File Allocation Table (FAT) works.

The three main functions that this article will deal with are:

1. rewind() – return the file pointer to the beginning;
2. fseek() – position the file pointer;
3. ftell() – return the current offset of the file pointer.

Each of these functions operates on the C file pointer, which is just the offset from the start of the file, and can be positioned at will. All read/write operations take place at the current position of the file pointer.

The rewind() Function:

The rewind() function can be used in sequential or random access C file programming, and simply tells the file system to position the file pointer at the start of the file. Any error flags will also be cleared, and no value is returned.

While useful, the companion function, fseek(), can also be used to reposition the file pointer at will, including the same behavior as rewind().

Using fseek() and ftell() to Process Files:

The fseek() function is most useful in random access files where either the record (or block) size is known, or there is an allocation system that denotes the start and end positions of records in an index portion of the file. The fseek() function takes three parameters:

1. FILE * f – the file pointer;
2. long offset – the position offset;
3. int origin – the point from which the offset is applied.

The origin parameter can be one of three values

1. SEEK_SET – from the start;
2. SEEK_CUR – from the current position;
3. SEEK_END – from the end of the file.

So, the equivalent of rewind() would be:
fseek(f, 0, SEEK_SET);

By a similar token, if the programmer wanted to append a record to the end of the file, the pointer could be repositioned thus:
fseek(f, 0, SEEK_END);

Since fseek() returns an error code (0 for no error) the stdio library also provides a function that can be called to find out the current offset within the file:

long offset = ftell(FILE * f)

This enables the programmer to create a simple file marker (before updating a record for example), by storing the file position in a variable, and then supplying it to a call to fseek:

long file_marker = ftell(f);

File Processing Functions:

fseek(f, file_marker, SEEK_SET);

Of course, if the programmer knows the size of each record or block, arithmetic can be used. For example, to rewind to the start of the current record, a function call such as the following would suffice:

fseek(f, 0 – record_size, SEEK_CURR);

With these three functions, the C programmer can manipulate both sequential and random access files, but should always remember that positioning the file pointer is absolute. In other words, if fseek is used to position the pointer in a read/write file, then writing will overwrite existing data, permanently.

Error handling:

The standard I/O functions maintain two indicators with each open stream to show the end-of-file and error status of the stream. These can be interrogated and set by the following functions:

void clearerr(FILE *stream);
int feof(FILE *stream);
int ferror(FILE *stream);
void perror(const char *s);

1. Clearer clears the error and EOF indicators for the stream.
2. Feof returns non-zero if the stream's EOF indicator is set, zero otherwise.
3. Ferror returns non-zero if the stream's error indicator is set, zero otherwise.
4. Perror prints a single-line error message on the program's standard output, prefixed by the string pointed to by s, with a colon and a space appended. The error message is determined by the value of errno and is intended to give some explanation of the condition causing the error.

For example, this program produces the error message shown as below:

#include <stdio.h>

```
#include <stdlib.h>
main()
{
fclose(stdout);
if(fgetc(stdout) >= 0)
{
fprintf(stderr, "What - no error!\n");
exit(EXIT_FAILURE);
}
perror("fgetc");
exit(EXIT_SUCCESS);
}
/* Result */
fgetc: Bad file number
```

CONCLUDING REMARKS

This chapter has explained the procedure for opening files and storing information in them. The various I/O functions related to high level and low level file disk operations have been elaborated with programming examples. Command line arguments are arguments from which command prompt of the operating system is described.

Chapter 12

DYNAMIC MEMORY ALLOCATION

ABSTRACT

This chapter covers the Static and Dynamic memory allocation concepts. It also covers the memory allocation process.
Outline:

- Static memory Allocation
- Dynamic memory Allocation

12.1. STATIC MEMORY ALLOCATION

Static allocation is when the amount of space for an array or some other construct is determined at compile-time. The disadvantage of this is that we don't always know how big an array we need until the program is run.

With static allocation, if we wanted a char array label to be able to hold various *strings*, then we would have to determine the length of all of the strings that would be held in label and then make that array large enough to accommodate the largest string.

For example, if we need to store labels like: "Single", "Married (J)", "Married (S)", and "Head of Household"... *What would be the size of the array needed to hold these things?*

    char label[??];

In some cases, we can't determine the maximum size at compile-time. For example, suppose labels are entered by user when the program is run, there is no size that we can choose for the array while ensuring that the user doesn't type in something longer.

12.2. DYNAMIC MEMORY ALLOCATION

Dynamic Memory Allocation, refers to Memory allocations process, Allocating a block of memory, Allocating multiple blocks of memory, Releasing the used space and to alter the size of allocated memory.

In programming we may come across situations where we may have to deal with data, which is dynamic in nature. The number of data items may change during the execution of a program. The number of customers in queue can increase or decrease during the process at any time. When the list grows, we need to allocate more memory space to accommodate additional data items. Such situations can be handled more easily by using dynamic techniques. Dynamic data items at run time, help in optimizing file usage of storage space.

On other hand, the process of allocating memory at run time is known as dynamic memory allocation. Although c does not inherently have this facility, there are four library routines which allow this function. Many languages permit a programmer to specify an array size at run time. Such languages have the ability to calculate and assign during execution, the memory space required by the variables in the program. But c inherently does not have this facility but supports it with memory management functions, which can be used to allocate and free memory during the program execution. The following functions are used in c for purpose of memory management.

Function	Task
malloc	Allocates memory requests size of bytes and returns a pointer to the Ist byte of allocated space
calloc	Allocates space for an array of elements initializes them to zero and returns a pointer to the memory
free	Frees previously allocated space
realloc	Modifies the size of previously allocated space.

Memory allocations process:

According to the conceptual view, the program instructions and global and static variable in a permanent storage area and local area variables are stored in stacks. The memory space that is located between these two regions is

Dynamic Memory Allocation

available for dynamic allocation during the execution of the program. The free memory region is called the heap. The size of heap keeps changing when a program is executed due to creation and death of variables that are local for functions and blocks. Therefore it is possible to encounter memory overflow during dynamic allocation process. In such situations, the memory allocation functions mentioned above will return a null pointer.

Allocating a block of memory:

A block mf memory may be allocated using the function malloc. The malloc function reserves a block of memory of specified size and returns a pointer of type void. This means that we can assign it to any type of pointer. It takes the following form:

ptr=(cast-type*)malloc(byte-size);

ptr is a pointer of type cast-type the malloc returns a pointer (of cast type) to an area of memory with size byte-size.

Example: x=(int*)malloc(100*sizeof(int));

On successful execution of this statement a memory equivalent to 100 times the area of int bytes is reserved and the address of the first byte of memory allocated is assigned to the pointer x of type int

Allocating multiple blocks of memory:

Calloc is another memory allocation function that is normally used to request multiple blocks of storage each of the same size and then sets all bytes to zero. The general form of calloc is:

ptr=(cast-type*) calloc(n,elem-size);

The above statement allocates contiguous space for n blocks each size of elements. All bytes are initialized to zero and a pointer to the first byte of the allocated region is returned. If there is not enough space a null pointer is returned.

Releasing the used space:

Compile time storage of a variable is allocated and released by the system in accordance with its storage class. With the dynamic runtime allocation, it is our responsibility to release the space when it is not required. The release of storage space becomes important when the storage is limited. When we no longer need the data we stored in a block of memory and we do not intend to use that block for storing any other information, we may release that block of memory for future use, using the free function.

free(ptr);

ptr is a pointer that has been created by using malloc or calloc.

To alter the size of allocated memory:
The memory allocated by using calloc or malloc might be insufficient or excess sometimes and in both the situations we can change the memory size already allocated with the help of the function realloc. This process is called reallocation of memory. The general statement of reallocation of memory is:

ptr=realloc(ptr,newsize);

This function allocates new memory space of size newsize to the pointer variable ptr ans returns a pointer to the first byte of the memory block. The allocated new block may be or may not be at the same region.

Example program for reallocation
```
#include< stdio.h >
#include< stdlib.h >
define NULL 0
main()
{
char *buffer;
/*Allocating memory*/
if((buffer=(char *) malloc(10))==NULL)
{
printf("Malloc failed\n");
exit(1);
}
printf("Buffer of size %d created \n,_msize(buffer));
strcpy(buffer,"Bangalore");
printf("\nBuffer contains:%s\n",buffer);
/*Reallocation*/
if((buffer=(char *)realloc(buffer,15))==NULL)
{
printf("Reallocation failed\n");
exit(1);
}
printf("\nBuffer size modified.\n");
printf("\nBuffer still contains: %s\n",buffer);
strcpy(buffer,"Mysore");
printf("\nBuffer now contains:%s\n",buffer);
```

/*freeing memory*/
free(buffer); }

CONCLUDING REMARKS

This chapter has covered the Static and Dynamic memory allocation concepts. It has also covered the memory allocation process.

APPENDIX A. EXERCISES FOR CRUISING YOUR TECHNICAL MIND

Write C programs to perform the following tasks.

Exercise 0:

Input two numbers and work out their sum, average and sum of the squares of the numbers.

Exercise 1:

Input and output your name, address and age to an appropriate structure.

Exercise 2:

Write a program that works out the largest and smallest values from a set of 10 input numbers.

Exercise 3:

Write a program to read a "float" representing a number of degrees Celsius, and print as a "float" the equivalent temperature in degrees Fahrenheit. Print your results in a form such as

100.0 degrees Celsius converts to 212.0 degrees Fahrenheit.

Exercise 4:

Write a program to print several lines (such as your name and address). You may use either several printf instructions, each with a newline character in it, or one printf with several newlines in the string.

Exercise 5:

Write a program to read a positive integer at least equal to 3, and print out all possible permutations of three positive integers less than or equal to this value.

Exercise 6:

Write a program to read a number of units of length (a float) and print out the area of a circle of that radius. Assume that the value of pi is 3.14159 (an appropriate declaration will be given to you by ceilidh - select setup).

Your output should take the form: The area of a circle of radius ... units is .... units.

If you want to be clever, and have looked ahead in the notes, print the message Error: Negative values not permitted. if the input value is negative.

Exercise 7:

Giving as input a floating (real) number of centimeters, print out the equivalent number of feet (integer) and inches (floating, 1 decimal), with the inches given to an accuracy of one decimal place.

Assume 2.54 centimeters per inch, and 12 inches per foot.

If the input value is 333.3, the output format should be:

333.3 centimeters is 10 feet 11.2 inches.

Exercise 8:

Giving as input an integer number of seconds, print as output the equivalent time in hours, minutes and seconds. Recommended output format is something like

7322 seconds is equivalent to 2 hours 2 minutes 2 seconds.

APPENDIX B.
MISCELLANEOUS QUESTION AND ANSWERS

EX:1
Main()
{
Int a,b=22,c=345;
a=b,c;
printf("%d",a);
}
OUTPUT : 22

EX:2
Main()
{
Int a,b=22,c=345;
a=(b,c);
printf("%d",a);
}
OUTPUT : 345

Notice the difference between the above two examples and the following upcoming example. You will notice a very small difference in the expression but this result in a major output change.

EX:3
Main()
{
Int a,b=22,c=345;

```
a=(c++,b,c++);
printf("%d",a,c);
}
```
OUTPUT : 346 347

Note:
The above expressions are evaluated from left to right obviously. But what is given as input will become big.

In the above example -1 I used the expression as a=b,c and in the next example it is used as a=(b,c). See the output of these examples. As said earlier it matters significantly.

Sometimes you can use like this by mistake. When the compiler knows it is wrong, you are on the safer side. But when the situation involves examples like above, you cannot easily find when and where the error occurred.

C is vast like a sea. It will become deepen as you gain the ability to swim. Note that care should be taken to handle all the programs and that you learn all the tips and tricks as well of the C language.

Can you use the function fprintf()to display the output on the screen?
Use it as: fprintf(stout, "Hello %s", name);
this line prints Hello on the console.

To print "Hello" in a file, put the file pointer in the place of stdout
EX: fprintf(fp, "Hello %s", name);

1. If you are using C language to implement the heterogeneous linked list, what pointer type will you use?

The heterogeneous linked list contains different data types in its nodes and we need a link, a pointer to connect them. It is not possible to use ordinary pointers for this. So we go for the void pointer. The Void pointer is capable of being a storing pointer to any type as it is a generic pointer type.

APPENDIX C. C QUESTIONS

Note : All the programs are tested under Turbo C/C++ compilers. It is assumed that,

1. Programs run under DOS environment,
2. The underlying machine is an x86 system,
3. Program is compiled using Turbo C/C++ compiler (32-Bit).

The program output may depend on the information based on this assumption (for example sizeof(int) = 2 is assumed).

Predict the output or error(s) for the following:

```
void main()
{
    int const * p=5;
    printf("%d",++(*p));
}
```

Answer:

Compiler error: Cannot modify a constant value.

Explanation:

p is a pointer to a "constant integer". But we tried to change the value of the "constant integer".

2.
```
main()
{
    char s[ ]="man";
    int i;
    for(i=0;s[ i ];i++)
    printf("\n%c%c%c%c",s[ i ],*(s+i),*(i+s),i[s]);
```

}
Answer:
  mmmm
  aaaa
  nnnn

Explanation:
s[i], *(i+s), *(s+i), i[s] are all different ways of expressing the same idea. Generally array name is the base address for that array. Here is the base address. i is the index number/displacement from the base address. So, indirecting it with * is same as s[i]. i[s] may be surprising. But in the case of C it is same as s[i].

3.
```
main()
{
    float me = 1.1;
    double you = 1.1;
    if(me==you)
printf("I love U");
else
        printf("I hate U");
}
```
Answer:
I hate U
Explanation:
For floating point numbers (float, double, long double) the values cannot be predicted exactly. Depending on the number of bytes, the precession with which the value is represented varies. Float takes 4 bytes and long double takes 10 bytes. So float stores 0.9 with less precision than long double.

Rule of Thumb:
Never compare or at-least be cautious when using floating point numbers with relational operators (== , >, <, <=, >=,!=) .

4.
```
Main()
    {
    static int var = 5;
    printf("%d ",var--);
```

```
        if(var)
                main();
    }
```
Answer:
5 4 3 2 1

Explanation:

When static storage class is given, it is initialized once. The change in the value of a static variable is retained even between the function calls. Main is also treated like any other ordinary function, which can be called recursively.

5.
```
main()
{
    int c[ ]={2.8,3.4,4,6.7,5};
    int j,*p=c,*q=c;
    for(j=0;j<5;j++) {
            printf(" %d ",*c);
            ++q;     }
    for(j=0;j<5;j++){
printf(" %d ",*p);
++p;       }
}
```

Answer:
 2 2 2 2 2 2 3 4 6 5

Explanation:

Initially pointer c is assigned to both p and q. In the first loop, since only q is incremented and not c, the value 2 will be printed 5 times. In the second loop p itself is incremented. So the values 2 3 4 6 5 will be printed.

6.
```
main()
{
    extern int i;
    i=20;
printf("%d",i);
}
```

Answer:
Linker Error : Undefined symbol '_i'
Explanation:
    extern storage class in the following declaration,
        extern int i;
specifies to the compiler that the memory for i is allocated in some other program and that address will be given to the current program at the time of linking. But linker finds that no other variable of name i is available in any other program with memory space allocated for it. Hence a linker error has occurred .

7.
```
main()
{
    int i=-1,j=-1,k=0,l=2,m;
    m=i++&&j++&&k++||l++;
    printf("%d %d %d %d %d",i,j,k,l,m);
}
```
Answer:
    0 0 1 3 1
Explanation :
Logical operations always give a result of 1 or 0 . And also the logical AND (&&) operator has higher priority over the logical OR (||) operator. So the expression 'i++ && j++ && k++' is executed first. The result of this expression is 0 (-1 && -1 && 0 = 0). Now the expression is 0 || 2 which evaluates to 1 (because OR operator always gives 1 except for '0 || 0' combination- for which it gives 0). So the value of m is 1. The values of other variables are also incremented by 1.

8.
```
main()
{
    char *p;
    printf("%d %d ",sizeof(*p),sizeof(p));
}
```

Answer:
    1 2
Explanation:

The sizeof() operator gives the number of bytes taken by its operand. P is a character pointer, which needs one byte for storing its value (a character). Hence sizeof(*p) gives a value of 1. Since it needs two bytes to store the address of the character pointer sizeof(p) gives 2.

9.
```
main()
{
    int i=3;
    switch(i)
    {
    default:printf("zero");
    case 1: printf("one");
            break;
    case 2:printf("two");
            break;
    case 3: printf("three");
            break;
    }
}
```
Answer :
three
Explanation :
The default case can be placed anywhere inside the loop. It is executed only when all other cases do not match.

10.
```
main()
{
    printf("%x",-1<<4);
}
```
Answer:
fff0
Explanation :
-1 is internally represented as all 1's. When left shifted four times the least significant 4 bits are filled with 0's. The %x format specifier specifies that the integer value be printed as a hexadecimal value.

11.
```
main()
{
 char string[]="Hello World";
     display(string);
}
void display(char *string)
{
    printf("%s",string);
}
```
Answer:
Compiler Error: Type mismatch in redeclaration of function display
Explanation:
In the third line, when the function display is encountered, the compiler doesn't know anything about the function display. It assumes the arguments and return types to be integers, (which is the default type). When it sees the actual function display, the arguments and types contradict with what was assumed previously. Hence a compile time error occurs.

12.
```
main()
{
    int c=- -2;
    printf("c=%d",c);
}
```
Answer:
        c=2;

Explanation:
Here unary minus (or negation) operator is used twice. Same mathematical rules apply here, i.e., minus * minus= plus.

Note:
However you cannot give like --2. Because -- operator can only be applied to variables as a decrement operator (e.g., i--). 2 is a constant and not a variable.

13.
```
#define int char
main()
{
```

```
    int i=65;
    printf("sizeof(i)=%d",sizeof(i));
}
```

Answer:
                sizeof(i)=1

Explanation:
Since the #define replaces the string int by the macro char

14.
```
main()
{
int i=10;
i=!i>14;
Printf ("i=%d",i);
}
```
Answer:
i=0

Explanation:
In the expression !i>14 , NOT (!) operator has more precedence than ' >' symbol. ! is a unary logical operator. !i (!10) is 0 (not of true is false). 0>14 is false (zero).

15.
```
#include<stdio.h>
main()
{
char s[]={'a','b','c','\n','c','\0'};
char *p,*str,*str1;
p=&s[3];
str=p;
str1=s;
printf("%d",++*p + ++*str1-32);
}
```
Answer:
77

Explanation:
   p is pointing to character '\n'. str1 is pointing to character 'a' ++*p. "p is pointing to '\n' and that is incremented by one." the ASCII value of '\n' is 10,

which is then incremented to 11. The value of ++*p is 11. ++*str1, str1 is pointing to 'a' that is incremented by 1 and it becomes 'b'. ASCII value of 'b' is 98.

Now performing (11 + 98 – 32), we get 77("M");
So we get the output 77 :: "M" (Ascii is 77).

16.
```
#include<stdio.h>
main()
{
int a[2][2][2] = { {10,2,3,4}, {5,6,7,8} };
int *p,*q;
p=&a[2][2][2];
*q=***a;
printf("%d----%d",*p,*q);
}
```
Answer:
SomeGarbageValue---1

Explanation:
p=&a[2][2][2] you declare only two 2D arrays, but you are trying to access the third 2D(which you have not declared) it will print garbage values. *q=***a starting address of a is assigned integer pointer. Now q is pointing to starting address of a. If you print *q, it will print the first element of 3D array.

17.
```
#include<stdio.h>
main()
{
struct xx
 {
  int x=3;
  char name[]="hello";
 };
struct xx *s;
printf("%d",s->x);
printf("%s",s->name);
}
```
Answer:
Compiler Error

Explanation:
You should not initialize variables in declaration

18.
```
#include<stdio.h>
main()
{
struct xx
{
int x;
struct yy
{
char s;
    struct xx *p;
};
struct yy *q;
};
}
```
Answer:
Compiler Error
Explanation:
The structure yy is nested within structure xx. Hence, the elements of yy are to be accessed through the instance of structure xx, which needs an instance of yy to be known. If the instance is created after defining the structure the compiler will not know about the instance relative to xx. Hence for the nested structure yy you have to declare member.

19.
```
main()
{
printf("\nab");
printf("\bsi");
printf("\rha");
}
```
Answer:
hai
Explanation:
\n - newline
\b - backspace

\r - linefeed

20.
```
main()
{
int i=5;
printf("%d%d%d%d%d",i++,i--,++i,--i,i);
}
```
Answer:
45545

Explanation:
The arguments in a function call are pushed into the stack from left to right. The evaluation is done by popping out from the stack and it is from right to left, hence the result.

21.
```
#define square(x) x*x
main()
{
int i;
i = 64/square(4);
printf("%d",i);
}
```
Answer:
64

Explanation:
the macro call square(4) will substituted by 4*4 so the expression becomes i = 64/4*4. Since / and * has equal priority the expression will be evaluated as (64/4)*4 i.e. 16*4 = 64

22.
```
main()
{
char *p="hai friends",*p1;
p1=p;
while(*p!='\0') ++*p++;
printf("%s %s",p,p1);
}
```
Answer:
ibj!gsjfoet

Explanation:
  ++*p++ will be parse in the given order
*p that is value at the location currently pointed by p will be taken
++*p the retrieved value will be incremented
when ; is encountered the location will be incremented that is p++ will be executed

Hence, in the while loop initial value pointed by p is 'h', it is changed to 'i' by executing ++*p and the pointer moves to point 'a' which is similarly changed to 'b' and so on. Similarly blank space is converted to '!'. Thus, the obtained value in p becomes "ibj!gsjfoet" and since p reaches '\0' and p1 points to p thus p1 does not print anything.

23.
```
#include <stdio.h>
#define a 10
main()
{
#define a 50
printf("%d",a);
}
```
Answer:
50
Explanation:
The preprocessor directives can be redefined anywhere in the program. So the most recently assigned value will be taken.

24.
```
#define clrscr() 100
main()
{
clrscr();
printf("%d\n",clrscr());
}
```
Answer:
100
Explanation:
Preprocessor executes as a separate pass before the execution of the compiler. So textual replacement of clrscr() to 100 occurs. The input program to compiler looks like this :

```
main()
{
100;
printf("%d\n",100);
}
```
Note:

100; is an executable statement but with no action. So it doesn't pose any problem

25.
```
main()
{
printf("%p",main);
}
```
Answer:
                Some address will be printed.

Explanation:

Function names are just addresses (just like array names are addresses).

main() is also a function. So the address of the function main will be printed. %p in printf specifies that the argument is an address. They are printed as hexadecimal numbers.

26.
```
main()
{
clrscr();
}
clrscr();
```

Answer:

No output/error

Explanation:

The first clrscr() occurs inside a function. So it becomes a function call. In the second clrscr(); it is a function declaration (because it is not inside any function).

27.
    enum colors {BLACK,BLUE,GREEN}

```
main()
{
printf("%d..%d..%d",BLACK,BLUE,GREEN);
return(1);
}
```
Answer:
0..1..2
Explanation:
enum assigns numbers starting from 0, if not explicitly defined.

29)
```
void main()
{
char far *farther,*farthest;

printf("%d..%d",sizeof(farther),sizeof(farthest));

}
```
Answer:
4..2
Explanation:
    the second pointer is of char type and not a far pointer

30)
```
main()
{
int i=400,j=300;
printf("%d..%d");
}
```
Answer:
400..300
Explanation:
printf takes the values of the first two assignments of the program. Any number of printf's may be given. All of them take only the first two values. If more number of assignments are given in the program, then printf will take garbage values.

31)
```
main()
{
char *p;
```

```
p="Hello";
printf("%c\n",*&*p);
}
```
Answer:
H
Explanation:
* is a dereference operator and is a reference operator. They can be applied any number of times provided the application is meaningful. Here p points to the first character in the string "Hello". *p dereferences it and so its value is H. Again & references it to an address and * dereferences it to the value H.

```
32) main()
{
int i=1;
while (i<=5)
{
printf("%d",i);
if (i>2)
    goto here;
i++;
}
}
fun()
{
here:
printf("PP");
}
```
Answer:
Compiler error: Undefined label 'here' in function main
Explanation:
Labels have functions scope, in other words the scope of the labels is limited to functions . The label 'here' is available in function fun() Hence it is not visible in function main.

```
33) main()
{
static char names[5][20]={"pascal","ada","cobol","fortran","perl"};
int i;
```

```
    char *t;
    t=names[3];
    names[3]=names[4];
    names[4]=t;
    for (i=0;i<=4;i++)
        printf("%s",names[i]);
}
```
Answer:
Compiler error: Lvalue required in function main
Explanation:
Array names are pointer constants. So they cannot be modified.

34)
```
void main()
{
    int i=5;
    printf("%d",i++ + ++i);
}
```
Answer:
Output Cannot be predicted exactly.
Explanation:
Side effects are involved in the evaluation of i

35)
```
void main()
{
    int i=5;
    printf("%d",i+++++i);
}
```
Answer:
Compiler Error
Explanation:
The expression i+++++i is parsed as i ++ ++ + i which is an illegal combination of operators.

36)
```
#include<stdio.h>
main()
{
int i=1,j=2;
switch(i)
```

{
case 1: printf("GOOD");
    break;
case j: printf("BAD");
    break;
}
}
Answer:
Compiler Error: Constant expression required in function main.
Explanation:
The case statement can have only constant expressions (this implies that we cannot use variable names directly and so an error).
Note:
Enumerated types can be used in case statements.

37) main()
{
int i;
printf("%d",scanf("%d",&i)); // value 10 is given as input here
}
Answer:
1
Explanation:
Scanf returns a number of items successfully read and not 1/0. Here 10 is given as input which should have been scanned successfully. So number of items read is 1.

38) #define f(g,g2) g##g2
main()
{
int var12=100;
printf("%d",f(var,12));
}
Answer:
100

39) main()
{
int i=0;

```
for(;i++;printf("%d",i)) ;
printf("%d",i);
}
```
Answer:
    1
Explanation:
before entering into the for loop the checking condition is "evaluated". Here it evaluates to 0 (false) and comes out of the loop, and i is incremented (note the semicolon after the for loop).

```
40) #include<stdio.h>
main()
{
char s[]={'a','b','c','\n','c','\0'};
char *p,*str,*str1;
p=&s[3];
str=p;
str1=s;
printf("%d",++*p + ++*str1-32);
}
```

Answer:
M
Explanation:
p is pointing to character '\n'.str1 is pointing to character 'a' ++*p meAnswer:"p is pointing to '\n' and that is incremented by one." the ASCII value of '\n' is 10. then it is incremented to 11. the value of ++*p is 11. ++*str1 meAnswer:"str1 is pointing to 'a' that is incremented by 1 and it becomes 'b'. ASCII value of 'b' is 98. both 11 and 98 is added and result is subtracted from 32.
    i.e. (11+98-32)=77("M");

```
41) #include<stdio.h>
main()
{
struct xx
{
int x=3;
char name[]="hello";
```

```
};
struct xx *s=malloc(sizeof(struct xx));
printf("%d",s->x);
printf("%s",s->name);
}
```
Answer:
Compiler Error
Explanation:
Initialization should not be done for structure members inside the structure declaration

42)
```
#include<stdio.h>
main()
{
struct xx
   {
       int x;
       struct yy
       {
       char s;
       struct xx *p;
       };
       struct yy *q;
   };
}
```
Answer:
Compiler Error
Explanation:
in the end of nested structure yy a member has to be declared.

43)
```
main()
{
 extern int i;
 i=20;
 printf("%d",sizeof(i));
}
```
Answer:
Linker error: undefined symbol '_i'.

Explanation:
extern declaration specifies that the variable i is defined somewhere else. The compiler passes the external variable to be resolved by the linker. So the compiler doesn't find an error. During linking, the linker searches for the definition of i. Since it is not found the linker flags an error.

```
44) main()
{
printf("%d", out);
}
int out=100;
```
Answer:
Compiler error: undefined symbol out in function main.
Explanation:
The rule is that a variable is available for use from the point of declaration. Even though a is a global variable, it is not available for main. Hence an error.

```
45) main()
{
 extern out;
 printf("%d", out);
}
 int out=100;
```
Answer:
100
    Explanation:
This is the correct way of writing the previous program.

```
46) main()
{
 show();
}
void show()
{
 printf("I'm the greatest");
}
```
Answer:
Compier error: Type mismatch in redeclaration of show.

Explanation:
When the compiler sees the function show, it doesn't know anything about it. So the default return type (ie, int) is assumed. But when compiler sees the actual definition of show, a mismatch occurs since it is declared as void. Hence the error.

The solutions are as follows:
1. declare void show() in main() .
2. define show() before main().
3. declare extern void show() before the use of show().

47) main( )
{
int a[2][3][2] = {{{2,4},{7,8},{3,4}},{{2,2},{2,3},{3,4}}};
printf("%u %u %u %d \n",a,*a,**a,***a);
    printf("%u %u %u %d \n",a+1,*a+1,**a+1,***a+1);
}
Answer:
100, 100, 100, 2
114, 104, 102, 3
Explanation:
          The given array is a 3-D one. It can also be viewed as a 1-D array.

2	4	7	8	3	4	2	2	2	3	3	4
100 102 104 106 108 110 112 114 116 118 120 122

thus, for the first printf statement a, *a, **a give the address of first element since the indirection ***a gives the value. Hence, the first line of the output.
    for the second printf a+1 increases in the third dimension thus pointing to value at 114, *a+1 increments in second dimension thus pointing to 104, **a +1 increments the first dimension thus pointing to 102 and ***a+1 first gets the value at first location and then increments it by 1. Hence, the output.

48) main( )
{
int a[ ] = {10,20,30,40,50},j,*p;
for(j=0; j<5; j++)
    {

```
printf("%d" ,*a);
a++;
 }
p = a;
for(j=0; j<5; j++)
 {
printf("%d " ,*p);
p++;
 }
 }
```
Answer:
Compiler error: lvalue required.

Explanation:
Error is in line with statement a++. The operand must be an lvalue and may be of any of scalar types for any operator, and array name when subscripted is an lvalue. Array name simply is a non-modifiable lvalue.

49) main( )
```
{
static int a[ ] = {0,1,2,3,4};
int *p[ ] = {a,a+1,a+2,a+3,a+4};
int **ptr = p;
ptr++;
printf("\n %d %d %d", ptr-p, *ptr-a, **ptr);
*ptr++;
printf("\n %d %d %d", ptr-p, *ptr-a, **ptr);
*++ptr;
printf("\n %d %d %d", ptr-p, *ptr-a, **ptr);
++*ptr;
    printf("\n %d %d %d", ptr-p, *ptr-a, **ptr);
}
```
Answer:
    111
    222
    333
    344

Explanation:
Let us consider the array and the two pointers with some address

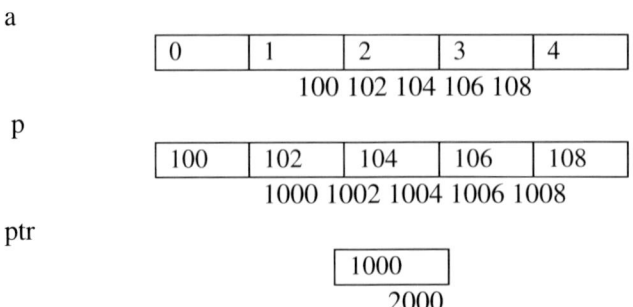

After execution of the instruction ptr++ value in ptr becomes 1002, if scaling factor for integer is 2 bytes. Now ptr – p is value in ptr – starting location of array p, (1002 – 1000) / (scaling factor) = 1, *ptr – a = value at address pointed by ptr – starting value of array a, 1002 has a value 102 so the value is (102 – 100)/(scaling factor) = 1, **ptr is the value stored in the location pointed by the pointer of ptr = value pointed by value pointed by 1002 = value pointed by 102 = 1. Hence the output of the firs printf is 1, 1, 1.

After execution of *ptr++ increments value of the value in ptr by scaling factor, so it becomes1004. Hence, the outputs for the second printf are ptr – p = 2, *ptr – a = 2, **ptr = 2.

After execution of *++ptr increments value of the value in ptr by scaling factor, so it becomes1004. Hence, the outputs for the third printf are ptr – p = 3, *ptr – a = 3, **ptr = 3.

After execution of ++*ptr value in ptr remains the same, the value pointed by the value is incremented by the scaling factor. So the value in array p at location 1006 changes from 106 10 108,. Hence, the outputs for the fourth printf are ptr – p = 1006 – 1000 = 3, *ptr – a = 108 – 100 = 4, **ptr = 4.

50) main( )
{
char *q;
int j;
for (j=0; j<3; j++) scanf("%s" ,(q+j));
for (j=0; j<3; j++) printf("%c" ,*(q+j));
for (j=0; j<3; j++) printf("%s" ,(q+j));
}
Explanation:
Here we have only one pointer to type char and since we take input in the same pointer, we keep writing over in the same location, each time shifting the

pointer value by 1. Suppose the inputs are MOUSE, TRACK and VIRTUAL. Then for the first input the pointer starts at location 100 then the input one is stored as

M	O	U	S	E	\0

When the second input is given, the pointer is incremented as j value becomes 1, so the input is filled in memory starting from 101.

M	T	R	A	C	K	\0

The third input starts filling from the location 102

M	T	V	I	R	T	U	A	L	\0

This is the final value stored.
The first printf prints the values at the position q, q+1 and q+2 = M T V
The second printf prints three strings starting from locations q, q+1, q+2
i.e., MTVIRTUAL, TVIRTUAL and VIRTUAL.

51) main( )
{
void *vp;
char ch = 'g', *cp = "goofy";
int j = 20;
vp = &ch;
printf("%c", *(char *)vp);
vp = &j;
printf("%d",*(int *)vp);
vp = cp;
printf("%s",(char *)vp + 3);
}
Answer:
    g20fy
Explanation:
Since a void pointer is used it can be type casted to any other type pointer. vp = &ch stores the address of char ch and the next statement prints the value stored in vp after type casting it to the proper data type pointer the output is

'g'. Similarly the output from second printf is '20'. The third printf statement type casts it to print the string from the 4th value and hence the output is 'fy'.

52) main ( )
{
static char *s[ ] = {"black", "white", "yellow", "violet"};
char **ptr[ ] = {s+3, s+2, s+1, s}, ***p;
p = ptr;
**++p;
printf("%s",*--*++p + 3);
}
Answer:
   ck
Explanation:
In this problem we have an array of char pointers pointing to start of 4 strings. Then we have ptr which is a pointer to a pointer of type char and a variable p which is a pointer to a pointer to a pointer of type char. p holds the initial value of ptr, i.e. p = s+3. The next statement increment value in p by 1, thus new value of p = s+2. In the printf statement the expression is evaluated *++p causes gets value s+1 then the pre decrement is executed and we get s+1 − 1 = s. The indirection operator now gets the value from the array of s and adds 3 to the starting address. The string is printed starting from this position. Thus, the output is 'ck'.

53) main()
{
int i, n;
char *x = "girl";
n = strlen(x);
*x = x[n];
for(i=0; i<n; ++i)
{
printf("%s\n",x);
x++;
}
}
Answer:
(blank space)
irl

rl
l

Explanation:
Here a string (a pointer to char) is initialized with a value "girl". The strlen function returns the length of the string, thus n has a value 4. The next statement assigns value at the nth location ('\0') to the first location. Now the string becomes "\0irl". Now the printf statement prints the string after each iteration it increments it starting position. Loop starts from 0 to 4. The first time x[0] = '\0' hence it prints nothing and pointer value is incremented. The second time it prints from x[1] i.e., "irl" and the third time it prints "rl" and the last time it prints "l" and the loop terminates.

54) int i,j;
for(i=0;i<=10;i++)
{
j+=5;
assert(i<5);
}

Answer:
Runtime error: Abnormal program termination.
     assert failed (i<5), <file name>,<line number>

Explanation:
asserts are used during debugging to make sure that certain conditions are satisfied. If assertion fails, the program will terminate reporting the same. After debugging use,
 #undef NDEBUG
and this will disable all the assertions from the source code. Assertion is a good debugging tool to make use of.

55) main()
{
int i=-1;
+i;
printf("i = %d, +i = %d \n",i,+i);
}

Answer:
i = -1, +i = -1

Explanation:
Unary + is the only dummy operator in C. Where-ever it comes you can just ignore it just because it has no effect in the expressions (hence the name dummy operator).

56) What are the files which are automatically opened when a C file is executed?
Answer:
stdin, stdout, stderr (standard input,standard output,standard error).

57) What will be the position of the file marker?
    a: fseek(ptr,0,SEEK_SET);
    b: fseek(ptr,0,SEEK_CUR);

Answer :
    a: The SEEK_SET sets the file position marker to the starting of the file.
    b: The SEEK_CUR sets the file position marker to the current position of the file.

58) main()
```
{
char name[10],s[12];
scanf(" \"%[^\"]\"",s);
}
```
How scanf will execute?
Answer:
First it checks for the leading white space and discards it. Then it matches with a quotation mark and then it reads all characters upto another quotation mark.

59) What is the problem with the following code segment?
```
while ((fgets(receiving array,50,file_ptr)) != EOF)
    ;
```
Answer & Explanation:
fgets returns a pointer. So the correct end of file check is checking for != NULL.

60) main()
   {
   main();
   }
Answer:
Runtime error : Stack overflow.
Explanation:
main function calls itself again and again. Each time the function is called its return address is stored in the call stack. Since there is no condition to terminate the function call, the call stack overflows at runtime. So it terminates the program and results in an error.

61) main()
   {
   char *cptr,c;
   void *vptr,v;
   c=10; v=0;
   cptr=&c; vptr=&v;
   printf("%c%v",c,v);
   }
Answer:
Compiler error (at line number 4): size of v is Unknown.
Explanation:
You can create a variable of type void * but not of type void, since void is an empty type. In the second line you are creating variable vptr of type void * and v of type void. Hence an error.

62) main()
   {
   char *str1="abcd";
   char str2[]="abcd";
   printf("%d %d %d",sizeof(str1),sizeof(str2),sizeof("abcd"));
   }
Answer:
2 5 5
Explanation:
In the first sizeof, str1 is a character pointer so it gives you the size of the pointer variable. In second sizeof the name str2 indicates the name of the array

whose size is 5 (including the '\0' termination character). The third sizeof is similar to the second one.

63) ```
main()
{
char not;
not=!2;
printf("%d",not);
}
```
Answer:
0

Explanation:
! is a logical operator. In C the value 0 is considered to be the boolean value FALSE, and any non-zero value is considered to be the boolean value TRUE. Here 2 is a non-zero value so TRUE. !TRUE is FALSE (0) so it prints 0.

64) ```
#define FALSE -1
#define TRUE 1
#define NULL 0
main() {
if(NULL)
        puts("NULL");
else if(FALSE)
        puts("TRUE");
else
        puts("FALSE");
}
```
Answer:
TRUE

Explanation:
The input program to the compiler after processing by the preprocessor is,
```
main(){
        if(0)
                puts("NULL");
        else if(-1)
                puts("TRUE");
        else
                puts("FALSE");
```

}

Preprocessor doesn't replace the values given inside the double quotes. The check by if condition is boolean value false so it goes to else. In second if -1 is boolean value true hence "TRUE" is printed.

65) main()
```
{
int k=1;
printf("%d==1 is ""%s",k,k==1?"TRUE":"FALSE");
}
```
Answer:
1==1 is TRUE
Explanation:
When two strings are placed together (or separated by white-space) they are concatenated (this is called as "stringization" operation). So the string is as if it is given as "%d==1 is %s". The conditional operator(?:) evaluates to "TRUE".

66) main()
```
{
int y;
scanf("%d",&y); // input given is 2000
if( (y%4==0 && y%100 != 0) || y%100 == 0 )
 printf("%d is a leap year");
else
 printf("%d is not a leap year");
}
```
Answer:
2000 is a leap year
Explanation:
An ordinary program to check if it is a leap year or not.

67) #define max 5
```
   #define int arr1[max]
   main()
   {
   typedef char arr2[max];
   arr1 list={0,1,2,3,4};
   arr2 name="name";
```

```
printf("%d %s",list[0],name);
}
```
Answer:

Compiler error (in the line arr1 list = {0,1,2,3,4})

Explanation:

arr2 is declared as type array of size 5 of characters. So it can be used to declare the variable name of the type arr2. But it is not the case of arr1. Hence an error.

Rule of Thumb:

#defines are used for textual replacement whereas typedefs are used for declaring new types.

68)
```
int i=10;
main()
{
extern int i;
    {
    int i=20;
        {
            const volatile unsigned i=30;
            printf("%d",i);
        }
    printf("%d",i);
    }
printf("%d",i);
}
```
Answer:

30,20,10

Explanation:

'{' introduces new block and thus the new scope. In the innermost block i is declared as,

　　　const volatile unsigned

which is a valid declaration. i is assumed of type int. So printf prints 30. In the next block, i has value 20 and so printf prints 20. In the outermost block, i is declared as extern, so no storage space is allocated for it. After compilation is over, the linker resolves it to global variable i (since it is the only variable visible there). So it prints i's value as 10.

69) main()
    {
        int *j;
        {
            int i=10;
            j=&i;
        }
        printf("%d",*j);
    }
Answer:
10
Explanation:
The variable i is a block level variable and the visibility is inside that block only. But the lifetime of i is lifetime of the function so it lives upto the exit of main function. Since the i is still allocated space, *j prints the value stored in i since j points i.

70) main()
    {
        int i=-1;
        -i;
        printf("i = %d, -i = %d \n",i,-i);
    }
Answer:
i = -1, -i = 1
Explanation:
-i is executed and this execution doesn't affect the value of i. In printf first you just print the value of i. After that the value of the expression -i = -(-1) is printed.

71) #include<stdio.h>
main()
{
const int i=4;
float j;
j = ++i;
printf("%d %f", i,++j);
}

Answer:
Compiler error
 Explanation:
i is a constant. you cannot change the value of a constant

72) #include<stdio.h>
main()
{
int a[2][2][2] = { {10,2,3,4}, {5,6,7,8} };
int *p,*q;
p=&a[2][2][2];
*q=***a;
printf("%d..%d",*p,*q);
}
Answer:
garbagevalue..1
Explanation:
p=&a[2][2][2] you declare only two 2D arrays. but you are trying to access the third 2D(which you have not declared) it will print garbage values. *q=***a starting address of a is assigned integer pointer. now q is pointing to starting address of a. If you print *q meAnswer: it will print first element of 3D array.

73) #include<stdio.h>
main()
{
register i=5;
char j[]= "hello";
printf("%s %d",j,i);
}
Answer:
hello 5
Explanation:
if you declare i as register, compiler will treat it as ordinary integer and it will take integer value. i value may be stored either in register or in memory.

74) main()
{
    int i=5,j=6,z;

```
       printf("%d",i+++j);
       }
```
Answer:
11
Explanation:
the expression i+++j is treated as (i++ + j)

76)
```
struct aaa{
struct aaa *prev;
int i;
struct aaa *next;
};
main()
{
 struct aaa abc,def,ghi,jkl;
 int x=100;
 abc.i=0;abc.prev=&jkl;
 abc.next=&def;
 def.i=1;def.prev=&abc;def.next=&ghi;
 ghi.i=2;ghi.prev=&def;
 ghi.next=&jkl;
 jkl.i=3;jkl.prev=&ghi;jkl.next=&abc;
 x=abc.next->next->prev->next->i;
 printf("%d",x);
}
```
Answer:
2

Explanation:
All above statements form a double circular linked list;
abc.next->next->prev->next->i
this one points to "ghi" node the value of at particular node is 2.

77)
```
struct point
 {
 int x;
 int y;
 };
struct point origin,*pp;
```

```
main()
{
pp=&origin;
printf("origin is(%d%d)\n",(*pp).x,(*pp).y);
printf("origin is (%d%d)\n",pp->x,pp->y);
}
```

Answer:
origin is(0,0)
origin is(0,0)
Explanation:
pp is a pointer to structure. we can access the elements of the structure either with arrow mark or with indirection operator.
Note:
Since structure point is globally declared x & y are initialized as zeroes

78)
```
main()
{
 int i=_l_abc(10);
     printf("%d\n",--i);
}
int _l_abc(int i)
{
 return(i++);
}
```
Answer:
9
Explanation:
return(i++) it will first return i and then increments. i.e. 10 will be returned.

79)
```
main()
{
 char *p;
 int *q;
 long *r;
 p=q=r=0;
 p++;
 q++;
```

r++;
printf("%p...%p...%p",p,q,r);
}
Answer:
0001...0002...0004
Explanation:
++ operator when applied to pointers increments address according to their corresponding data-types.

```
80) main()
{
 char c=' ',x,convert(z);
 getc(c);
 if((c>='a') && (c<='z'))
 x=convert(c);
 printf("%c",x);
}
convert(z)
{
 return z-32;
}
```
Answer:
Compiler error
Explanation:
declaration of convert and format of getc() are wrong.

```
81) main(int argc, char **argv)
{
 printf("enter the character");
 getchar();
 sum(argv[1],argv[2]);
}
sum(num1,num2)
int num1,num2;
{
 return num1+num2;
}
```
Answer:
Compiler error.

Explanation:
argv[1] & argv[2] are strings. They are passed to the function sum without converting to integer values.

82) # include <stdio.h>
int one_d[]={1,2,3};
main()
{
 int *ptr;
 ptr=one_d;
 ptr+=3;
 printf("%d",*ptr);
}
Answer:
garbage value
Explanation:
ptr pointer is pointing to out of the array range of one_d.

83) # include<stdio.h>
aaa() {
 printf("hi");
 }
bbb(){
 printf("hello");
 }
ccc(){
 printf("bye");
 }
main()
{
 int (*ptr[3])();
 ptr[0]=aaa;
 ptr[1]=bbb;
 ptr[2]=ccc;
 ptr[2]();
}
Answer:
bye

Explanation:

ptr is array of pointers to functions of return type int.ptr[0] is assigned to address of the function aaa. Similarly ptr[1] and ptr[2] for bbb and ccc respectively. ptr[2]() is in effect of writing ccc(), since ptr[2] points to ccc.

85) #include<stdio.h>
main()
{
FILE *ptr;
char i;
ptr=fopen("zzz.c","r");
while((i=fgetch(ptr))!=EOF)
printf("%c",i);
}
Answer:
contents of zzz.c followed by an infinite loop
    Explanation:
The condition is checked against EOF, it should be checked against NULL.

86) main()
{
 int i =0;j=0;
 if(i && j++)
    printf("%d..%d",i++,j);
printf("%d..%d,i,j);
}
Answer:
0..0
Explanation:
The value of i is 0. Since this information is enough to determine the truth value of the boolean expression, the statement following the if statement is not executed. The values of i and j remain unchanged and get printed.

87) main()
{
 int i;
 i = abc();
 printf("%d",i);

}
abc()
{
_AX = 1000;
}
Answer:
1000
Explanation:
Normally the return value from the function is through information from the accumulator. Here _AH is the pseudo global variable denoting the accumulator. Hence, the value of the accumulator is set at 1000 so the function returns value 1000.

88) int i;
   main(){
int t;
for (t=4;scanf("%d",&i)-t;printf("%d\n",i))
   printf("%d--",t--);
   }
   // If the inputs are 0,1,2,3 find the o/p
Answer:
   4--0
         3--1
         2--2
Explanation:
Let us assume some x= scanf("%d",&i)-t the values during execution
            will be,
t i x
4 0 -4
3 1 -2
2 2 0

89) main(){
int a= 0;int b = 20;char x =1;char y =10;
if(a,b,x,y)
printf("hello");
}
Answer:
hello

Explanation:

The comma operator has associativity from left to right. Only the rightmost value is returned and the other values are evaluated and ignored. Thus the value of last variable y is returned to check in if. Since it is a non zero value if becomes true so, "hello" will be printed.

```
90) main(){
    unsigned int i;
    for(i=1;i>-2;i--)
            printf("c aptitude");
}
```
Explanation:

i is an unsigned integer. It is compared with a signed value. Since the both types don't match, signed is promoted to unsigned value. The unsigned equivalent of -2 is a huge value so condition becomes false and control comes out of the loop.

91) In the following pgm add a stmt in the function fun such that the address of
'a' gets stored in 'j'.
```
main(){
int * j;
void fun(int **);
fun(&j);
}
void fun(int **k) {
int a =0;
/* add a stmt here*/
}
```
Answer:
            *k = &a
Explanation:
            The argument of the function is a pointer to a pointer.

92) What are the following notations of defining functions known as?
i. int abc(int a,float b)
        {
    /* some code */
        }

ii. int abc(a,b)
  int a; float b;
      {
      /* some code*/
      }
Answer:
i. ANSI C notation
ii. Kernighan & Ritche notation

93) main()
{
char *p;
p="%d\n";
    p++;
    p++;
    printf(p-2,300);
}
Answer:
    300
Explanation:
The pointer points to % since it is incremented twice and again decremented by 2, it points to '%d\n' and 300 is printed.

94) main(){
char a[100];
a[0]='a';a[1]]='b';a[2]='c';a[4]='d';
abc(a);
}
abc(char a[]){
a++;
    printf("%c",*a);
a++;
printf("%c",*a);
}
Explanation:
The base address is modified only in function and as a result a points to 'b' then after incrementing to 'c' so bc will be printed.

95) func(a,b)

```
int a,b;
{
 return( a= (a==b) );
}
main()
{
int process(),func();
printf("The value of process is %d !\n ",process(func,3,6));
}
process(pf,val1,val2)
int (*pf) ();
int val1,val2;
{
return((*pf) (val1,val2));
 }
```
Answer:
The value if process is 0 !

Explanation:

The function 'process' has 3 parameters - 1, a pointer to another function 2 and 3, integers. When this function is invoked from main, the following substitutions for formal parameters take place: func for pf, 3 for val1 and 6 for val2. This function returns the result of the operation performed by the function 'func'. The function func has two integer parameters. The formal parameters are substituted as 3 for a and 6 for b. since 3 is not equal to 6, a==b returns 0. therefore the function returns 0 which in turn is returned by the function 'process'.

96)
```
void main()
{
    static int i=5;
    if(--i){
            main();
            printf("%d ",i);
    }
}
```
Answer:
0 0 0 0

Explanation:
The variable "I" is declared as static, hence memory for I will be allocated only once, as it encounters the statement. The function main() will be called recursively unless I becomes equal to 0, and since main() is recursively called, the value of static I i.e., 0 will be printed every time the control is returned.

97) void main()
{
    int k=ret(sizeof(float));
    printf("\n here value is %d",++k);
}
int ret(int ret)
{
    ret += 2.5;
    return(ret);
}

Answer:
Here value is 7

Explanation:
The int ret(int ret), i.e., the function name and the argument name can be the same.

First, the function ret() is called in which the sizeof(float) i.e., 4 is passed, after the first expression the value in ret will be 6, as ret is integer and hence the value stored in ret will have implicit type conversion from float to int. The ret is returned in main() it is printed after and preincrement.

98) void main()
{
    char a[]="12345\0";
    int i=strlen(a);
    printf("here in 3 %d\n",++i);
}

Answer:
here in 3 6

Explanation:
    The char array 'a' will hold the initialized string, whose length will be counted from 0 till the null character. Hence the 'I' will hold the value equal to 5, after the pre-increment in the printf statement, the 6 will be printed.

99) void main()
{
    unsigned giveit=-1;
    int gotit;
    printf("%u ",++giveit);
    printf("%u \n",gotit=--giveit);
}
Answer:
 0 65535
Explanation:

100)   void main()
{
    int i;
    char a[]="\0";
    if(printf("%s\n",a))
            printf("Ok here \n");
    else
            printf("Forget it\n");
}
Answer:
 Ok here
Explanation:
Printf will return how many characters it prints. Hence printing a null character returns 1 which makes the if statement true, thus "Ok here" is printed.

101)   void main()
{
    void *v;
    int integer=2;
    int *i=&integer;
    v=i;
    printf("%d",(int*)*v);
}
Answer:
Compiler Error. We cannot apply indirection on type void*.

Explanation:
Void pointer is a generic pointer type. No pointer arithmetic can be done on it. Void pointers are normally used for,
Passing generic pointers to functions and returning such pointers.
As a intermediate pointer type.
Used when the exact pointer type will be known at a later point of time.

102)   void main()
{
    int i=i++,j=j++,k=k++;
    printf("%d%d%d",i,j,k);
}
Answer:
Garbage values.
Explanation:
An identifier is available to use in the program code from the point of its declaration.
So expressions such as i = i++ are valid statements. The i, j and k are automatic variables and so they contain some garbage value. Garbage in is garbage out (GIGO).

103)   void main()
{
    static int i=i++, j=j++, k=k++;
    printf("i = %d j = %d k = %d", i, j, k);
}
Answer:
i = 1 j = 1 k = 1
Explanation:
Since static variables are initialized to zero by default.

104)   a)void main()
{
    while(1)
    {
            if(printf("%d",printf("%d")))
                    break;
            else
                    continue;

            }
    }
    Answer:
    Garbage values
    Explanation:
    The inner printf executes first to print some garbage value. The printf returns no of characters printed and this value also cannot be predicted. Still the outer printf prints something and returns a non-zero value. So it encounters the break statement and comes out of the while statement.

    104)b)   main()
    {
        unsigned int i=10;
        while(i-->=0)
                printf("%u ",i);
    }
    Answer:
        10 9 8 7 6 5 4 3 2 1 0 65535 65534…..
    Explanation:
    Since i is an unsigned integer it can never become negative. So the expression i-- >=0 will always be true, leading to an infinite loop.

    105)   #include<conio.h>
    main()
    {
        int x,y=2,z,a;
        if(x=y%2) z=2;
        a=2;
        printf("%d %d ",z,x);
    }
     Answer:
    Garbage-value 0
    Explanation:
    The value of y%2 is 0. This value is assigned to x. The condition reduces to if (x) or in other words if(0) and so z goes uninitialized.
        Thumb Rule: Check all control paths to write a bug free code.

    106)   main()
    {

```
    int a[10];
    printf("%d",*a+1-*a+3);
}
```
Answer:
4

Explanation:
*a and -*a cancels out. The result is as simple as 1 + 3 = 4 !

107)   #define prod(a,b) a*b
```
main()
{
    int x=3,y=4;
    printf("%d",prod(x+2,y-1));
}
```
Answer:
10

Explanation:
The macro expands and evaluates to as:
x+2*y-1 => x+(2*y)-1 => 10

108)   main()
```
{
    unsigned int i=65000;
    while(i++!=0);
    printf("%d",i);
}
```
Answer:
1

Explanation:
Note the semicolon after the while statement. When the value of i becomes 0 it comes out of while loop. Due to post-increment on i the value of i while printing is 1.

109)   main()
```
{
    int i=0;
    while(+(+i--)!=0)
        i-=i++;
    printf("%d",i);
```

}
Answer:
-1

Explanation:
Unary + is the only dummy operator in C. So it has no effect on the expression and now the while loop is, while (i--!=0) which is false and so breaks out of while loop. The value −1 is printed due to the post-decrement operator.

113)   main()
{
    float f=5,g=10;
    enum{i=10,j=20,k=50};
    printf("%d\n",++k);
    printf("%f\n",f<<2);
    printf("%lf\n",f%g);
    printf("%lf\n",fmod(f,g));
}

Answer:
Line no 5: Error: Lvalue required
Line no 6: Cannot apply leftshift to float
Line no 7: Cannot apply mod to float

Explanation:
Enumeration constants cannot be modified, so you cannot apply ++.
Bit-wise operators and % operators cannot be applied on float values.
fmod() is to find the modulus values for floats as % operator is for ints.

110)   main()
{
    int i=10;
    void pascal f(int,int,int);
    f(i++,i++,i++);
    printf(" %d",i);
}
void pascal f(integer :i,integer:j,integer :k)
{

write(i,j,k);
}
Answer:
Compiler error: unknown type integer
Compiler error: undeclared function write
Explanation:
Pascal keyword doesn't mean that pascal code can be used. It means that the function follows Pascal argument passing mechanism in calling the functions.

111)   void pascal f(int i,int j,int k)
{
printf("%d %d %d",i, j, k);
}
void cdecl f(int i,int j,int k)
{
printf("%d %d %d",i, j, k);
}
main()
{
    int i=10;
f(i++,i++,i++);
    printf(" %d\n",i);
i=10;
f(i++,i++,i++);
printf(" %d",i);
}
Answer:
10 11 12 13
12 11 10 13
Explanation:
Pascal argument passing mechanism forces the arguments to be called from left to right. cdecl is the normal C argument passing mechanism where the arguments are passed from right to left.

112) What is the output of the program given below

main()
{

signed char i=0;
for(;i>=0;i++) ;
printf("%d\n",i);
}
Answer
                -128
Explanation

Notice the semicolon at the end of the for loop. THe initial value of the i is set to 0. The inner loop executes to increment the value from 0 to 127 (the positive range of char) and then it rotates to the negative value of -128. The condition in the for loop fails and so comes out of the for loop. It prints the current value of i that is -128.

113) main()
{
unsigned char i=0;
for(;i>=0;i++) ;
printf("%d\n",i);
}
Answer
      infinite loop
Explanation

The difference between the previous question and this one is that the char is declared to be unsigned. So the i++ can never yield negative value and i>=0 never becomes false so that it can come out of the for loop.

114) main()
{
char i=0;
for(;i>=0;i++) ;
printf("%d\n",i);
}
Answer:
            Behavior is implementation dependent.
Explanation:

The detail if the char is signed/unsigned by default is implementation dependent. If the implementation treats the char to be signed by default the program will print –128 and terminate. On the other hand if it considers char to be unsigned by default, it goes to infinite loop.

Rule:
You can write programs that have implementation dependent behavior. But don't write programs that depend on such behavior.

115)
Is the following statement a declaration/definition. Find what does it mean?
int (*x)[10];
Answer
   Definition.
   x is a pointer to array of(size 10) integers.
   Apply clock-wise rule to find the meaning of this definition.

116). What is the output for the program given below :-
typedef enum errorType{warning, error, exception,}error;
main()
{
error g1;
g1=1;
printf("%d",g1);
}
Answer
            Compiler error: Multiple declaration for error
Explanation
The name error is used in two meanings. One means that it is a enumerator constant with value 1. The other use is that it is a type name (due to typedef) for enum errorType. Given a situation the compiler cannot distinguish the meaning of error to know in what sense the error is used:
      error g1;
g1=error;
      // which error it refers in each case?
When the compiler can distinguish between usages then it will not issue error (in pure technical terms, names can only be overloaded in different namespaces).
   Note: the extra comma in the declaration,
   enum errorType{warning, error, exception,}
   is not an error. An extra comma is valid and is provided just for programmer's convenience.

117)
```
typedef struct error{int warning, error, exception;}error;
main()
{
error g1;
g1.error =1;
printf("%d",g1.error);
}
```

Answer
   1

Explanation

The three usages of name errors can be distinguishable by the compiler at any instance, so valid (they are in different namespaces).

Typedef struct error{int warning, error, exception;}error;

This error can be used only by preceding the error by struct kayword as in:

struct error someError;

typedef struct error{int warning, error, exception;}error;

This can be used only after . (dot) or -> (arrow) operator preceded by the variable name as in :

g1.error =1;
    printf("%d",g1.error);
        typedef struct error{int warning, error, exception;}error;

This can be used to define variables without using the preceding struct keyword as in:

error g1;

Since the compiler can perfectly distinguish between these three usages, it is perfectly legal and valid.

Note:-

This code is given here to just explain the concept behind. In real programming don't use such overloading of names. It reduces the readability of the code. Possible doesn't mean that we should use it!

118)   #ifdef something
```
int some=0;
#endif
main()
{
int thing = 0;
```

```
printf("%d %d\n", some ,thing);
}
```
Answer:

          Compiler error : undefined symbol some

Explanation:

This is a very simple example for conditional compilation. The name something is not already known to the compiler making the declaration

   int some = 0;

effectively removed from the source code.

119)   #if something == 0
```
int some=0;
#endif
main()
{
int thing = 0;
printf("%d %d\n", some ,thing);
}
```

Answer

        0 0

Explanation

This code is to show that preprocessor expressions are not the same as the ordinary expressions. If a name is not known the preprocessor treats it to be equal to zero.

120) What is the output for the following program
```
    main()
{
int arr2D[3][3];
printf("%d\n", ((arr2D==* arr2D)&&(* arr2D == arr2D[0])) );
}
```
Answer

1

Explanation

This is due to the close relation between the arrays and pointers. N dimensional arrays are made up of (N-1) dimensional arrays.

   arr2D is made up of a 3 single arrays that contain 3 integers each.

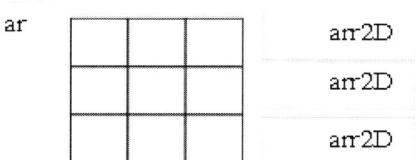

The name arr2D refers to the beginning of all the 3 arrays. *arr2D refers to the start of the first 1D array (of 3 integers) that is the same address as arr2D. So the expression (arr2D == *arr2D) is true (1).

Similarly, *arr2D is nothing but *(arr2D + 0), adding a zero doesn't change the value/meaning. Again arr2D[0] is the another way of telling *(arr2D + 0). So the expression (*(arr2D + 0) == arr2D[0]) is true (1).

Since both parts of the expression evaluates to true the result is true(1) and the same is printed.

121) void main()
{
if(~0 == (unsigned int)-1)
printf("You can answer this if you know how values are represented in memory");
}

Answer:
You can answer this if you know how values are represented in memory
Explanation:
~ (tilde operator or bit-wise negation operator) operates on 0 to produce all ones to fill the space for an integer. −1 is represented in unsigned value as all 1's and so both are equal.

122) int swap(int *a,int *b)
{
*a=*a+*b;*b=*a-*b;*a=*a-*b;
}
main()
{
    int x=10,y=20;
    swap(&x,&y);
    printf("x= %d y = %d\n",x,y);
}

Answer:
x = 20 y = 10

Explanation:
This is one way of swapping two values. Simple checking will help understand this.

123)   main()
{
char *p = "ayqm";
printf("%c",++*(p++));
}
Answer:
b

124)   main()
{
   int i=5;
   printf("%d",++i++);
}
Answer:
Compiler error: Lvalue required in function main

Explanation:
++i yields an rvalue. For postfix ++ to operate an lvalue is required.

125)   main()
{
char *p = "ayqm";
char c;
c = ++*p++;
printf("%c",c);
}

Answer:
b

Explanation:
There is no difference between the expression ++*(p++) and ++*p++. Parenthesis just works as a visual clue for the reader to see which expression is first evaluated.

126)
```
int aaa() {printf("Hi");}
int bbb(){printf("hello");}
iny ccc(){printf("bye");}
main()
{
int ( * ptr[3]) ();
ptr[0] = aaa;
ptr[1] = bbb;
ptr[2] =ccc;
ptr[2]();
}
```
Answer:
bye

Explanation:
int (* ptr[3])() says that ptr is an array of pointers to functions that takes no arguments and returns the type int. By the assignment ptr[0] = aaa; it means that the first function pointer in the array is initialized with the address of the function aaa. Similarly, the other two array elements also get initialized with the addresses of the functions bbb and ccc. Since ptr[2] contains the address of the function ccc, the call to the function ptr[2]() is same as calling ccc(). So it results in printing "bye".

127)
```
main()
{
int i=5;
printf("%d",i=++i ==6);
}
```
Answer:
1
Explanation:
The expression can be treated as i = (++i==6), because == is of higher precedence than = operator. In the inner expression, ++i is equal to 6 yielding true(1). Hence the result.

128)   main()
{
          char p[ ]="%d\n";
p[1] = 'c';
printf(p,65);
}
Answer:
A
Explanation:
Due to the assignment p[1] = 'c' the string becomes, "%c\n". Since this string becomes the format string for printf and ASCII value of 65 is 'A', the same gets printed.

129)   void (* abc(int, void (*def) ())) ();
Answer:
  abc is a ptr to a function which takes 2 parameters .(a). an integer variable.(b). a ptrto a funtion which returns void. The return type of the function is void.
Explanation:
          Apply the clock-wise rule to find the result.

130)   main()
{
while (strcmp("some","some\0"))
printf("Strings are not equal\n");
   }
Answer:
No output
Explanation:
Ending the string constant with \0 explicitly makes no difference. So "some" and "some\0" are equivalent. So, strcmp returns 0 (false) hence breaking out of the while loop.

131)   main()
{
char str1[] = {'s','o','m','e'};
char str2[] = {'s','o','m','e','\0'};
while (strcmp(str1,str2))
printf("Strings are not equal\n");

}
Answer:
"Strings are not equal"
"Strings are not equal"
….

Explanation:

If a string constant is initialized explicitly with characters, '\0' is not appended automatically to the string. Since str1 doesn't have null termination, it treats whatever the values that are in the following positions as part of the string until it randomly reaches a '\0'. So str1 and str2 are not the same, hence the result.

132)   main()
{
int i = 3;
for (;i++=0;) printf("%d",i);
}
Answer:
Compiler Error: Lvalue required.

Explanation:

As we know, increment operators return rvalues and hence it cannot appear on the left hand side of an assignment operation.

133)   void main()
{
int *mptr, *cptr;
mptr = (int*)malloc(sizeof(int));
printf("%d",*mptr);
int *cptr = (int*)calloc(sizeof(int),1);
printf("%d",*cptr);
}
Answer:
garbage-value 0

Explanation:

The memory space allocated by malloc is uninitialized, whereas calloc returns the allocated memory space initialized to zeros.

134)   void main()
{

```
static int i;
while(i<=10)
(i>2)?i++:i--;
    printf("%d", i);
}
```
Answer:
            32767

Explanation:
Since i is static it is initialized to 0. Inside the while loop the conditional operator evaluates to false, executing i--. This continues till the integer value rotates to positive value (32767). The while condition becomes false and hence, comes out of the while loop, printing the i value.

135)   main()
{
          int i=10,j=20;
          j = i, j?(i,j)?i:j:j;
          printf("%d %d",i,j);
}
Answer:
10 10

Explanation:
        The Ternary operator (? :) is equivalent for if-then-else statement. So the question can be written as:
                if(i,j)
                {
if(i,j)
                    j = i;
                    else
                    j = j;
                }
          else   j = j;

136)
1. const char *a;
2. char* const a;
3. char const *a;
-Differentiate the above declarations.
Answer:

1. 'const' applies to char * rather than 'a' (pointer to a constant char)
  *a='F' : illegal
             a="Hi" : legal
2. 'const' applies to 'a' rather than to the value of a (constant pointer to char)
  *a='F' : legal
  a="Hi" : illegal
3. Same as 1.

137)   main()
{
       int i=5,j=10;
       i=i&=j&&10;
       printf("%d %d",i,j);
}
Answer:
1 10
Explanation:
The expression can be written as i=(i&=(j&&10)); The inner expression (j&&10) evaluates to 1 because j==10. i is 5. i = 5&1 is 1. Hence the result.

138)   main()
{
       int i=4,j=7;
       j = j || i++ && printf("YOU CAN");
       printf("%d %d", i, j);
}
Answer:
4 1
Explanation:
The boolean expression needs to be evaluated only if the truth value of the expression is not known. j is not equal to zero itself means that the expression's truth value is 1. Because it is followed by || and true || (anything) => true where (anything) will not be evaluated. So the remaining expression is not evaluated and so the value of i remains the same.
  Similarly when && operator is involved in an expression, when any of the operands becomes false, the whole expression's truth value becomes false and hence the remaining expression will not be evaluated.
       false && (anything) => false where (anything) will not be evaluated.

139)   main()
{
    register int a=2;
    printf("Address of a = %d",&a);
    printf("Value of a = %d",a);
}
Answer:
Compier Error: '&' on register variable
Rule to Remember:
    & (address of) operator cannot be applied on register variables.

140)   main()
{
    float i=1.5;
    switch(i)
    {
        case 1: printf("1");
        case 2: printf("2");
        default : printf("0");
    }
}
Answer:
Compiler Error: switch expression not integral
Explanation:
    Switch statements can be applied only to integral types.

141)   main()
{
    extern i;
    printf("%d\n",i);
    {
        int i=20;
        printf("%d\n",i);
    }
}
Answer:
Linker Error : Unresolved external symbol i

Explanation:
The identifier i is available in the inner block and so using extern has no use in resolving it.

142)   main()
{
          int a=2,*f1,*f2;
          f1=f2=&a;
          *f2+=*f2+=a+=2.5;
    printf("\n%d %d %d",a,*f1,*f2);
}
Answer:
16 16 16
Explanation:
f1 and f2 both refer to the same memory location a. So changes through f1 and f2 ultimately affects only the value of a.

143)   main()
{
    char *p="GOOD";
    char a[ ]="GOOD";
  printf("\n sizeof(p) = %d, sizeof(*p) = %d, strlen(p) = %d", sizeof(p), sizeof(*p), strlen(p));
      printf("\n sizeof(a) = %d, strlen(a) = %d", sizeof(a), strlen(a));
}
Answer:
          sizeof(p) = 2, sizeof(*p) = 1, strlen(p) = 4
          sizeof(a) = 5, strlen(a) = 4
Explanation:
          sizeof(p) => sizeof(char*) => 2
          sizeof(*p) => sizeof(char) => 1
          Similarly,
          sizeof(a) => size of the character array => 5

When sizeof operator is applied to an array it returns the sizeof the array and it is not the same as the sizeof the pointer variable. Here the sizeof(a) where a is the character array and the size of the array is 5 because the space necessary for the terminating NULL character should also be taken into account.

144)   #define DIM(array, type) sizeof(array)/sizeof(type)
main()
{
int arr[10];
printf("The dimension of the array is %d", DIM(arr, int));
}
Answer:
10
Explanation:
The size of integer array of 10 elements is 10 * sizeof(int). The macro expands to sizeof(arr)/sizeof(int) => 10 * sizeof(int) / sizeof(int) => 10.

145)   int DIM(int array[])
{
return sizeof(array)/sizeof(int);
}
main()
{
int arr[10];
printf("The dimension of the array is %d", DIM(arr));
}
Answer:
1
Explanation:
Arrays cannot be passed to functions as arguments and only the pointers can be passed. So the argument is equivalent to int * array (this is one of the very few places where [] and * usage are equivalent). The return statement becomes, sizeof(int *)/ sizeof(int) that happens to be equal in this case.

146)   main()
{
    static int a[3][3]={1,2,3,4,5,6,7,8,9};
    int i,j;
    static *p[]={a,a+1,a+2};
            for(i=0;i<3;i++)
        {
                    for(j=0;j<3;j++)
                    printf("%d\t%d\t%d\t%d\n",*(*(p+i)+j),
                    ((j+p)+i),*(*(i+p)+j),*(*(p+j)+i));

        }
}
Answer:

                        1 1 1 1
                        2 4 2 4
                3 7 3 7
                        4 2 4 2
                        5 5 5 5
                6 8 6 8
                        7 3 7 3
                        8 6 8 6
                9 9 9 9

Explanation:
                ((p+i)+j) is equivalent to p[i][j].

147)   main()
{
        void swap();
        int x=10,y=8;
        swap(&x,&y);
        printf("x=%d y=%d",x,y);
}
void swap(int *a, int *b)
{
*a ^= *b, *b ^= *a, *a ^= *b;
}

Answer:
x=10 y=8
Explanation:
Using ^ like this is a way to swap two variables without using a temporary variable and that too in a single statement.

Inside main(), void swap(); means that swap is a function that may take any number of arguments (not no arguments) and returns nothing. So this doesn't issue a compiler error by the call swap(&x,&y); that has two arguments.

This convention is historically due to pre-ANSI style (referred to as Kernighan and Ritchie style) style of function declaration. In that style, the swap function will be defined as follows,

```
void swap()
int *a, int *b
{
*a ^= *b, *b ^= *a, *a ^= *b;
}
```
where the arguments follow the (). So naturally the declaration for swap will look like, void swap() which means the swap can take any number of arguments.

148)
```
main()
{
    int i = 257;
    int *iPtr = &i;
    printf("%d %d", *((char*)iPtr), *((char*)iPtr+1) );
}
```
Answer:
    1 1

Explanation:
The integer value 257 is stored in the memory as, 00000001 00000001, so the individual bytes are taken by casting it to char * and get printed.

149)
```
main()
{
    int i = 258;
    int *iPtr = &i;
    printf("%d %d", *((char*)iPtr), *((char*)iPtr+1) );
}
```
Answer:
    2 1

Explanation:
The integer value 257 can be represented in binary as, 00000001 00000001. Remember that the INTEL machines are 'small-endian' machines. Small-endian means that the lower order bytes are stored in the higher memory addresses and the higher order bytes are stored in lower addresses. The integer value 258 is stored in memory as: 00000001 00000010.

150)
```
main()
{
    int i=300;
```

```
            char *ptr = &i;
            *++ptr=2;
            printf("%d",i);
}
```
Answer:
556

Explanation:

The integer value 300 in binary notation is: 00000001 00101100. It is stored in memory (small-endian) as: 00101100 00000001. Result of the expression *++ptr = 2 makes the memory representation as: 00101100 00000010. So the integer corresponding to it is 00000010 00101100 => 556.

151)   #include <stdio.h>
```
main()
{
char * str = "hello";
char * ptr = str;
char least = 127;
while (*ptr++)
 least = (*ptr<least ) ?*ptr :least;
printf("%d",least);
}
```
Answer:
0

Explanation:
After 'ptr' reaches the end of the string the value pointed by 'str' is '\0'. So the value of 'str' is less than that of 'least'. So the value of 'least' finally is 0.

152)   Declare an array of N pointers to functions returning pointers to functions returning pointers to characters?
Answer:
            (char*(*)( )) (*ptr[N])( );

153)   main()
```
{
struct student
{
char name[30];
```

```
struct date dob;
}stud;
struct date
{
int day,month,year;
};
scanf("%s%d%d%d", stud.rollno, &student.dob.day,
&student.dob.month, &student.dob.year);
}
```

Answer:

Compiler Error: Undefined structure date

Explanation:

Inside the struct definition of 'student' the member of type struct date is given. The compiler doesn't have the definition of date structure (forward reference is not allowed in C in this case) so it issues an error.

154)   main()
```
{
struct date;
struct student
{
char name[30];
struct date dob;
}stud;
struct date
    {
int day,month,year;
};
scanf("%s%d%d%d", stud.rollno, &student.dob.day, &student.dob.month, &student.dob.year);
}
```

Answer:

Compiler Error: Undefined structure date

Explanation:

Only declaration of struct date is available inside the structure definition of 'student' but to have a variable of type struct date the definition of the structure is required.

INDEX

A

access, 62, 67, 69, 75, 80, 83, 86, 92, 93, 94, 114, 138, 140
age, 1, 58, 60, 61, 91, 92, 103
alters, 31
apples, 64
aptitude, 145
arithmetic, 15, 16, 19, 24, 26, 67, 71, 94, 149
Arithmetic Operators, 15, 16, 24
Arrays of structure, 55, 60
Assignment Operators, 15, 16, 19

B

base, 2, 108, 146
Binary files, 86
Bitwise Operators, 15, 16, 21
branching, 27

C

C++, 2, 9, 69, 75, 77, 78, 107
Call by reference, 72
Call by value, 67, 72
casting, 8, 9, 79, 129, 170
category a, 38
Character, 52

classes, 8, 47, 86
colleges, ix
colon, 13, 20, 31, 94
Comma Operator, 22
communication, 87
compilation, 136, 158
complement, 25
complexity, 30
computer, 15, 28, 38, 59, 61, 67, 87, 92
Conditional branching, 27
Conditional or Ternary Operators, 15
Constant, 81, 122
convention, 169
customers, 98

D

data processing, 5
data structure, 51, 85, 87
data transfer, 72
Data type, 5, 6
database, 85
depth, 54
Dereference operator, 69
directives, 117
displacement, 108
double, 9, 21, 52, 80, 81, 108, 135, 139
Dynamic memory allocation, 97, 101

Index

E

Else if Ladder, 27
environment(s), 8, 107
Error handling, 94
execution, 12, 15, 23, 26, 27, 28, 30, 32, 47, 48, 68, 98, 99, 117, 128, 137, 144
Explicit, 9
Expressions, v, 15
External variable, 48

F

fgetchar(), 39
File, v, 85, 86, 87, 92, 94
first dimension, 126
Float, 8, 108
force, 26
Formatted I/O operations, 37
fputchar(), 39
fseek(), 87, 93
ftell(), 87, 93
Functions, v, 41, 43, 46, 55, 58, 87, 94

G

garbage, 114, 119, 138, 142, 150, 151, 163
getch(), 38, 39, 40, 83
getchar(), 23, 39, 89, 141
getche(), 37, 38, 39, 40
gets(), 37, 38, 39, 40
grouping, 24
guidance, vii

H

history, 1, 3
hybrid, 92

I

image, 85

Implicit, 8
indirection, 75, 126, 130, 140, 149
interface, 53
intervention, 42
issues, 172
iteration, 34, 131

K

kindergarten, 76

L

languages, 1, 2, 16, 47, 98
lifetime, 47, 48, 137
Logical Operators, 15, 16, 17
love, 108

M

man, 1, 107
management, 85, 86, 98
manipulation, 21
memory, 23, 43, 49, 52, 57, 61, 67, 68, 69, 75, 77, 79, 80, 81, 87, 97, 98, 99, 100, 101, 110, 129, 138, 147, 159, 163, 167, 170, 171
modulus, 16, 25, 153
multidimensional, 52
multiplication, 22, 24

N

Nested If, 27
nodes, 106
null, 52, 53, 79, 81, 99, 148, 149, 163
Null pointer, 79

O

ODD, 90
one dimension, 52

operating system, 2, 68, 87, 95
operations, 15, 16, 26, 37, 52, 53, 70, 85, 86, 88, 93, 95, 110
Operators, 15, 16, 19, 24

P

parents, xi
Pass by reference, 45
Pass by value, 44
permit, 98
Pointers, v, 65, 67, 69, 72, 74, 75, 77, 78, 79, 80, 81
Pointers and function, 67, 72
Program Control, v, 27
programming, 1, 5, 28, 43, 49, 69, 85, 92, 93, 95, 98, 157
programming languages, 28
prototype(s), 12, 44
putch(), 38, 39
putchar(), 37, 39
puts(), 39

Q

question mark, 20

R

radius, 103, 104
reading, 38, 86, 88, 91
reality, 68
Recursion, 41, 47
Reference operator, 68
Register, 48
Register variable, 48
Relational Operators, 15, 16, 17
requirements, 6, 77
reserves, 99
rewind(), 87, 93
root, 42
routines, 98
rules, 11, 14, 24, 30, 57, 112

S

scaling, 128
scope, 27, 36, 47, 48, 120, 136
showing, 34, 35
Special Operators, 15, 16, 22
specifications, 37, 38, 91
standard error, 132
Static, 48, 97, 101
Static variable, 48
storage, 5, 8, 47, 61, 62, 72, 85, 98, 99, 109, 110, 136
storage media, 85
structure(s), v, 11, 28, 55, 56, 57, 58, 59, 60, 61, 62, 65, 87, 103, 115, 124, 140, 172
style, 43, 76, 169
substitutes, 19
substitutions, 147
subtraction, 25
Switch, 30, 166

T

teaching experience, ix
techniques, 43, 86, 98
temperature, 103
terminals, 86
testing, 21
third dimension, 126
Typedef, 157

U

Unformatted I/O operations, 37
union(s), v, 55, 61, 63
updating, 94
USA, 1

V

variable(s), 5, 6, 7, 8, 9, 12, 13, 15, 17, 23, 38, 43, 44, 47, 48, 49, 50, 56, 57, 58, 60,

62, 63, 71, 80, 83, 98, 110, 112, 115, 150, 157, 166, 169

W

While loop, 33
worry, 7

Y

yield, 155